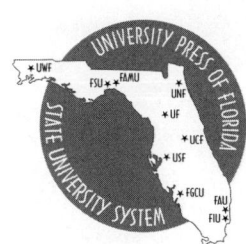

Florida A&M University, Tallahassee
Florida Atlantic University, Boca Raton
Florida Gulf Coast University, Ft. Myers
Florida International University, Miami
Florida State University, Tallahassee
University of Central Florida, Orlando
University of Florida, Gainesville
University of North Florida, Jacksonville
University of South Florida, Tampa
University of West Florida, Pensacola

Interpreting Narrative in the Novels of Samuel Beckett

Jonathan Boulter

University Press of Florida
Gainesville · Tallahassee · Tampa · Boca Raton
Pensacola · Orlando · Miami · Jacksonville · Ft. Myers

Copyright 2001 by Jonathan Boulter
Printed in the United States of America on acid-free paper
All rights reserved

06 05 04 03 02 01   6 5 4 3 2 1

Library of Congress Cataloging-in-Publication Data
Boulter, Jonathan, 1967–
Interpreting narrative in the novels of Samuel Beckett / Jonathan Boulter.
p. cm.
Includes bibliographical references and index.
ISBN 0-8130-2106-5 (acid-free paper)
1. Beckett, Samuel, 1906–1989—Fictional works. 2. Experimental fiction—
History and criticism. 3. Phenomenology in literature. 4. Philosophy in literature.
5. Narration (Rhetoric) I. Title.
PR6003.E282 Z5765 2001
823'.912—dc21   2001034073

The University Press of Florida is the scholarly publishing agency for the State
University System of Florida, comprising Florida A&M University, Florida Atlantic
University, Florida Gulf Coast University, Florida International University, Florida
State University, University of Central Florida, University of Florida, University of
North Florida, University of South Florida, and University of West Florida.

University Press of Florida
15 Northwest 15th Street
Gainesville, FL 32611-2079
http://www.upf.com

Page 151 is a continuation of this copyright page.

To Mitra Foroutan

and upon us all the silence will fall again, and settle, like dust of sand, on the arena, after the massacres
—Samuel Beckett, *The Unnamable*

Contents

Acknowledgments xi

Introduction 1

1. *Watt* 17

2. *Mercier and Camier* 38

3. *Molloy* 58

4. *Malone Dies* 81

5. *The Unnamable* 92

6. *How It Is* 109

Conclusion: The Dialogical Subject in *Endgame* and the Second Trilogy 124

Notes 135

Bibliography 143

Credits 151

Index 153

Acknowledgments

I wish to thank the following people and organizations:

Porter Abbott, for trenchant advice, generous criticism, and kind support

Michael Groden, for a superb reading of the original draft of the manuscript

Elizabeth Harvey, for being unstintingly generous with time and advice

Joel Faflak, for friendship and important conversations

Patrick Deane and Mary Neale, for help and encouragement

Anthony Brennan, for introducing me to the work of Samuel Beckett

The Social Sciences and Humanities Research Council of Canada, for a fellowship enabling me to prepare this manuscript

Introduction

And things, what is the correct attitude to adopt towards things?
—*The Unnamable*

This is an extraordinarily vibrant time for Beckett studies. The past years have seen the publication of several important critical studies, including H. Porter Abbott's *Beckett Writing Beckett: The Author in the Autograph* (1996), Richard Begam's *Samuel Beckett and the End of Modernity* (1996), and Daniel Katz's *Saying "I" No More* (1999), the publication of Beckett's *Collected Short Prose*, edited by Stanley Gontarski, and the publication of three critical biographies, Lois Gordon's *The World of Samuel Beckett, 1906–1946* (1996), James Knowlson's *Samuel Beckett* (1996), and Anthony Cronin's *Samuel Beckett: The Last Modernist* (1996).[1] The publication of this wealth of material speaks to Beckett's continuing importance and demonstrates the sense, not only among scholars of literature, philosophy, and literary theory but of the general public, that Beckett's work in some ways contains the central expression of the modernist and postmodernist experience. Beckett's work, from his novels to the drama, does not simply explore the fundamental anxieties of modernism but articulates these anxieties to ourselves: his work in some fashion *is* the modern experience. His novels and drama examine issues of suffering, death, and desire, the agonies of language and subjectivity in a postmetaphysical world; his work suggests fundamentally that the modern experience is one always mediated by an entropic language, a language of "worsening words" (104) that functions at a paradoxical "bounds of a boundless void"(116), as he puts it in *Worstward Ho*. These issues, ones he explored as early at the 1940s and continued to investigate until his death in 1989, are even more pressing as the new century unfolds. We still struggle with the issue of the *value* of language and its ability to communicate successfully the totality the modern world; we still struggle with the idea, central to Beckett, that the subject, the self, is not self-producing but is rather a product of ideological and linguistic forces that precede and exceed the subject; we still struggle urgently, in other words, with the attempt to *interpret* the world, to answer the central question of a philosophical hermeneutics: How does it stand toward me?

Interpreting Narrative in the Novels of Samuel Beckett reads the early to middle novels of Samuel Beckett (*Watt, Mercier and Camier, Molloy, Malone Dies, The Unnamable,* and *How It Is*) in the light of phenomenological-hermeneutical theory, primarily that of Hans-Georg Gadamer. Gadamer's philosophy of hermeneutics is crucial to this study because it makes clear that the experience of modernity is governed by the need for informed acts of interpretive judgment; his hermeneutics, in other words, translates modernity into theoretical terms and thus is the philosophical equivalent to Beckett's literary modernism. Moreover, Beckett and Gadamer have similar theoretical presentations of the subject (the self), a similarity that allows me to posit that Beckett's primary concern in his novels is the question of interpretation. Both Beckett and Gadamer suggest that the subject inhabits a world of discourse, both thematize the primacy of voice, and both, either implicitly or explicitly, thematize what I have at times called the ethics of dialogue. That is, both Gadamer and Beckett place the subject within a specific and, to use a word crucial to Beckett, *obligatory* system of dialogue. For Gadamer, understanding between two people arises only in the dynamics of dialogue, the give and take of what he calls the "hermeneutical conversation."[2] Beckett's subjects, as they are split into what in *Proust* he calls "separate and immanent dynamisms" (7), are compelled to engage *themselves* in a kind of aporetic dialogue, a failing universe of pure language that can never provide the final grounds of understanding. Gadamer's basic premise of the hermeneutical subject who engages the text (the person, the tradition, the history) in dialogue is formulated in a similar manner in the closed system of the Beckett text. Beckett's narrators, like Gadamer, explicitly argue that meaning, or the revelation of Being, can arise only through the structures of language; yet the Beckett narrator inhabits a closed universe in the sense that the language he uses only ever refers back to the grounds of its own failure.

The narrators of all the texts studied here are, as the narrator of Beckett's thirteenth Text for Nothing puts it, "born of the impossible voice" (140), a voice at once creating and created, speaking and spoken. The narrator is both subject of and to discourse. More precisely, he *is* discourse, as the narrator of *The Unnamable* says: "I'm in words, made of words, others' words . . . I'm all these words . . . with no ground for their settling" (386). As the texts explicitly thematize issues central to a philosophical hermeneutics (the notion of "world" as articulated by discourse, for instance), a hermeneutical and phenomenological reading of Beckett will function primarily to facilitate the text's disclosure of itself to the reader. The reader's responsibility to these texts, finally, is to place his or her interpretation against (or within) the interpretation already in place in the work: the reader of Beckett is thus by phenomenological necessity a radically self-conscious reader, and it is precisely this self-awareness that Beckett's work thematizes.

Indeed it has often been observed that Beckett's work seems always to have already anticipated the manner of its own reading. As Gary Handwerk puts it in "Alone with Beckett's Company" (not without a hint of frustration), "What can be said about Beckett's texts seems all too often to have been articulated already in Beckett's own critical writings or in the texts themselves" (65). Handwerk's frustration can be usefully seen as an initial observation of a basic hermeneutical principle: the text under scrutiny must be seen as providing the means of its own decipherment. The critic's role is to attempt to illustrate the interaction between the Beckett text and the reader so as to demonstrate how textual practice and theory engage in what may be called (somewhat laboriously) mutual self-articulation. One might suggest, in fact, that if our theories of reading seem to be anticipated by Beckett, we are penetrating to the heart of the interpretive matter. As Gadamer puts it with his usual disarming simplicity in *Philosophical Hermeneutics,* "The real power of hermeneutical consciousness is our ability to see what is questionable" (13).

Each chapter of this book explores the philosophical implications of this aporetic hermeneutics in relation to the narrating subject, whose readings of his world are always articulated *en abyme,* and to the actual reader, who is obligated to measure the economy of his or her own reading against the agonistic hermeneutic of the narrating subject. The question of interpretation in the novels thus is attenuated by the reader's awareness that his or her hermeneutic desire is always figured as a simulacrum of an originary reading itself logically "impossible" because never fully grounded. I thus analyze how Beckett's novels articulate what I have called an aporetic hermeneutic. Specifically, I explore how Beckett's texts can be read as at once confirming the preconditions of a Gadamerian hermeneutics and engaging in an interrogation and critique of that hermeneutics via the logic of aporia, via the breach of the subject in an unconfirmable discourse. The book is not intended to be a reading of Beckett through Gadamer but rather an extended exploration of the viability of hermeneutics in texts that resist even the first premises of a philosophical or revelatory hermeneutics.

This book is crucial to Beckett studies for several reasons. As a reading that logically emphasizes the presence of a reading subject, both thematized in the text and an actual reader following the progression of the hermeneutic, it builds on and supersedes seminal work whose first premises seem to have been largely passed over by the Beckett critical community. I am referring to a work such as H. Porter Abbott's *The Novels of Samuel Beckett,* which suggests that Beckett's novels thematize the reading process itself. My book is based centrally on an analysis of the process of reading in the firm belief that Beckett's novels not only thematize the reading process but in various ways are "about" the reader and the process of interpretation, or hermeneutics. The novels, in short, are about the philosophical-hermeneutical grounds of understanding, a theme that has received scant attention in Beckett criticism.

The Beckett community is caught between two extremes of reading Beckett's novels. The first, and most traditional, is what I and others call "allegorical" readings that stress formal similarities between Beckett's texts and any (and all, it sometimes seems) external systems of, for instance, philosophy or literature. This is a system of reading that essentially substitutes some stabilizing interpretive structure for the messy stuff of Beckett's text. At the other extreme are readings that emphasize the text and its textuality to such an extent as simply to repeat what seem to be Beckett's own first principles: the textuality of the subject, the endless play of the subject, the aporia of meaning. Although my instinctive sympathies are with the poststructuralist's emphasis on the difficulty of locating the subject and its meaning, it seems to me that such readings, exemplified, for instance, in Steven Connor's important *Repetition, Theory, and Text,* too easily deny the viability of interpretation and the reader, just as allegorical readings too easily move away from the difficulties inherent in the text. A medium avenue of reading is urgently needed here. A balance between extremes of textuality and extremes of allegory is required, a system that maintains its view of the textuality of the text and at once acknowledges the desire and temptation toward allegory or, indeed, reconfigures that desire in terms that keep the text in view.

Gadamer is important to my project as he provides the theoretical basis of my view of the relation between text and reader, which is properly understood in terms of mutuality and, importantly, dialectic. Gadamer writes: "Hermeneutic work is based on a polarity of familiarity and strangeness" (295). This dialectic of familiarity and strangeness is always at work in our hermeneutical conversation with the Beckett text. Semiotic moments of familiarity (moments when, for instance, Beckett's texts meet our generic expectations) hook the reader; however, threaded through these moments, for instance—and this is only one avenue Beckett will follow to "distance" his reader—are metatextual moments which, like Brecht's *Verfremdungseffekt,* force the reader into a new awareness of the ontology of the work and concomitantly into an awareness of his or her own role as reader/spectator. These moments of "awareness," crucially, exist simultaneously with moments of active hermeneutical inquiry to produce a vertiginous dialectic. We are drawn to the text in our desire to flesh out and give meaning to it; but we are simultaneously "distanced" by these metatextual moments and forced to see and read our interpretations "metahermeneutically," that is, only as interpretations, only as ethereal versions of a protean story. Thus an odd specularity is produced as the instability of the text begins to reflect the instability of the reading experience. The reader is, in fact, made into a shadow version of the characters within the novel or play whose own grasp on reality and meaning is tenuous and radically unsure.

It is at this moment that the reader begins to perceive fully the strange disquiet produced by the experience of reading. Concomitantly, it is at the moment of the reader's awareness of the provisional and protean nature of his or her interpretations that Beckett succeeds fully in destabilizing the reading subject *as* reading subject. The point I want to emphasize here is the absolute proximity of the reader to the text in the reading experience, a proximity noted by Gadamer and other philosophers in the late phenomenological tradition. In his essay "What Is a Text?" Paul Ricoeur notes: "What the interpreter says is a re-saying which reactivates what is said by the text" (164). This reawakening, and Gadamer too insists on this point, always already involves the reader's self-evaluation; my notion of metahermeneutics is in a way analogous to Ricoeur's notion of "appropriation":

> By 'appropriation' I understand this: that the interpretation of a text culminates in the self-interpretation of a subject who thenceforth understands himself better, understands himself differently, or simply begins to understand himself . . . understanding the text is not an

end in itself . . . in hermeneutic reflection—or in reflective hermeneutics—the constitution of the *self* is contemporaneous with the constitution of *meaning*. (158–59)

We might thus here be allowed to suggest that Beckett's texts, if they are "about" anything, are initially about the reader, who will ineluctably "find" himself "within" the text *as* (or in) the emblematic and specular reader.

Appropriation for Ricoeur is, as he notes in his essay "Appropriation," a "letting go" (191) of the subject: "It is always a question of entering into an alien work, of divesting oneself of the earlier 'me' in order to receive, as in play, the self conferred by the work itself" (190). Ricoeur's point is not to "lose" the self forever but to realize the degree and extent to which texts confer various reading subject positions. As the philosopher G. B. Madison notes in his *The Hermeneutics of Postmodernity*, Ricoeur theorizes a "desubjectivised" (92) subjectivity. Ricoeur and Beckett both realize the degree to which the subject as *reading* subject, that is, an hermeneut offering a reading of world, is always mediated to itself. Says Madison: "The presence of the subject to itself, which is the very definition of subjectivity and self-consciousness, is an indirect, *mediated* presence" (93). If I read Ricoeur and Beckett properly, the self (and text) can know itself only through its readings of itself, readings that can only *be* readings, thus provisional and subject to all the vagaries of any textual expression/interpretation. As Gadamer says, all experience—whether of text, of self, of world—is inevitably bound in the form of language: any understanding of text, self, and world (all of which inform the others) thus is linguistic in nature, hence the seeming endlessness of the hermeneutical conversation. Says Madison: "The reflecting subject in search of meaning, self-understanding, is a linguistic subject, a subject which is given to and which knows itself by means of the language it inhabits" (95).

Thus it seems important to use a strict hermeneutical approach when reading Beckett, as hermeneutics always theorizes the reader's processual self-consciousness as reader. It remains to highlight again the fact that the theoretical approach to texts defined by hermeneutics—its assignment of status to text and reader, its awareness of the subject as "text"—is always anticipated in Beckett's work. Thus a hermeneutical reading of Beckett will "simply" allow the text to "disclose" itself to the reader in the explicitly dialectical manner I have posited.

Beckett's texts provoke questions to which the specular reader is obliged to supply answers. What is the ontological status of the artwork and the audience's reading of that work? Can we place any firm trust in our readings of Beckett's fiction if the source of our readings reveals itself progressively to be fundamentally unstable? What are the implications of self-consciousness for Beckett's work and for a reading of that work? It is my contention that these questions—common enough in Beckett criticism—have not been properly contextualized. It is not enough merely to see the text as the site of an exploration of these questions. The Beckett text, precisely as its own hermeneutic is specular—that is, reflected in the reader—obliges the reader also to address these questions to him or herself and to his or her own hermeneutic. The point I wish to outline here finally is the degree to which our response to the Beckett text is an obligatory response, a response that, as it involves the reader's intimate awareness of him or herself as hermeneut, involves what I call an ethic. I am interested in exploring and expanding on the idea, suggested by Gadamer in *Truth and Method,* that hermeneutical action shares a qualitative similarity with ethical action. In a Beckettian context, in which, as I wish to suggest, an ethic is defined by its obligatory nature, and in which action undertaken by characters is in a very real sense echoed by the reader of that action, any hermeneutic will almost by definition, as it is obligatory, be "ethical."

A hermeneutic reading keeps the stuff of the text in focus by foregrounding the problematics of meaning. Hermeneutics, in short, acknowledges the primacy of text and the responsibilities of reading. It thus also thematizes, as Gadamer points out, an ethic implicit in the reading dynamic, an ethic founded in the exigencies of incomplete textual knowledge, an ethic that is absolutely central to the reading of Beckett. Ethics, as Aristotle suggests (and Aristotle is Gadamer's main source for his theme of hermeneutical ethics), comes into play only when the subject is faced with incomplete knowledge of how to proceed in a specific situation; indeed, if one is fully aware of all possible outcomes of a specific act, that act—and the apprehension of it—is not, according to Gadamer, an ethical situation. A complete ethical moment requires one to choose between possible outcomes, possible readings, possible meanings. Beckett's novels thematize ethical dilemmas insofar as they place the self-conscious reader in a reading situation the basic grounds of which are a priori denied, the outcome of which is often ambiguous, the logic of which seems occluded. In attempting to read through the various aporias of the Beckett novel, in attempting to make sense of this discursive universe, the reader is explicitly involved in an ethical moment. But this situation is ethical not only because of the general ambiguity of the discursive moment but because the reader is *obliged* to make some hermeneutical reading of it. By accepting the task of reading, the reader has accepted an obligation to the text and his or her reading of it. And indeed, obligation is a central theme of Beckett's novels. Often characters are obliged to "go on": they express to themselves a keen sense of obligation to articulate verbally their experience, to understand the reasons for their present predicament: "Where now? Who now? When now?" (*The Unnamable*). The characters' hermeneutical situation thus is uncannily similar to that of the reader: both character and reader are, to use Heidegger's idea, "thrown" into a (discursive) world without philosophical, narrative, or ontological signposts.

Like a great number of critics, I find Beckett's *Three Dialogues* to be of central importance to an understanding of the Beckettian ethos. It is of course the word "obligation" that is important here, a word used numerous times in the course of the "dialogues"; "B" prefers: "The expression that there is nothing to express, nothing with which to express, nothing from which to express, no power to express, no desire to express, together with the obligation to express" (139). Too often, I think, it is Beckett's "nothing" that is emphasized; his "obligation"—a crucial counterbalance to his nothing—is not given the priority it deserves. To posit the artist's expression as an obligation is of course to posit expression as at least partially an ethical act.[3] An obligation is, as J. Hillis Miller puts it in *The Ethics of Reading*, a matter of a "must" (I will return to this point). The interesting thing in "Three Dialogues" is "B's" coyness when it comes to articulating the moral force that impels the expression: "D: Why is [the artist] obliged to paint? B: I don't know" (142). Nevertheless the obligation to act—an obligation, crucially, shared by a great many of Beckett's characters (Watt, the Unnamable, Mouth, Krapp) and qualitatively different from the "compulsion" to act—is there: the obligatory act is an ethical act. And the ethical act in Beckett, I will argue, always orients itself toward the possibility of meaningfulness.

I arrive at this idea via the notion that (obligatory) action *qua* action is unreadable (meaningless) separated from its context: an action cannot logically be separated from context—any action thus has the possibility of being meaningful. As Madison points out, action and discourse (or as I will put it, action as discourse) are linked to meaningfulness: "The phenomenological fact—confirmed by economic observation—is that existence is meaningful in that it is unintelligible except in terms of meaningful action. No discourse, therefore, is possible which rejects the 'postulate of meaningfulness.' It is logically impossible to deny meaning, just as it is logically impossible to deny one's own existence as a subject" (101). I contend that the "context" of Beckett's meaningful or hermeneutic action (as discourse) is the reader, or, more precisely, the interaction between text and reader. Beckett in the *Three Dialogues* places the expressive concerns of his audience alongside those of his artist: "Among those whom we call great artists, I can think of none whose concern was not predominantly with his expressive possibilities, those of his vehicle, those of humanity" (142). Beckett's linking of the expressive concerns of the artist and those of his audience (humanity) allows me in part to suggest the degree to which the obligation of the artist is not qualitatively distinct from the audience's obligation to interpret expressively, in short that the obligation to express by the artist is met by the reader's obligation to interpret.

Here of course we arrive at the crux of the reader's critical aporia: the obligation to interpret texts that often and systematically resist any more than provisional understanding. I might formulate this obligatory dilemma borrowing from Hillis Miller who, in *Versions of Pygmalion*, asks what one's ethical-interpretive responsibilities are toward something that "cannot" be understood. This is a question often bypassed by the Beckett critic, who leaps wholesale over this very central semiological-epistemological problem and offers readings toward which only a gesture of instability is made. That is, it is conventional to suggest that readings of Beckett are difficult; it is more infrequent for one to acknowledge that this difficulty is the end of reading and that the problematics of *reading* are the critical-hermeneutical crux of the matter.

This book may be seen as an extended exploration of my conviction that a historically located hermeneutics is a foregrounding of the "act-consequence" (ethical) aspect of the critico-performative gesture. Gadamer himself acknowledges this foregrounding in his discussion of Aristotle in *Truth and Method*. He combines the Aristotelian notion of *phronesis* or practical judgment (moral knowledge) with the Platonic model of the dialogue to arrive at his paradigm of hermeneutical understanding.[4] The concept of *phronesis* fits the tenor of *Truth and Method*'s resistance to a rigorous methodological (read "scientific") understanding of the world, as *phronesis* must adapt itself to ever-changing (nonquantifiable) situations. Moral knowledge is part of the human sciences whose object "is man and what he knows of himself. But he knows himself as an acting being, and this kind of knowledge of himself does not seek to establish what is. An active being, rather, is concerned with what is not always the same but can also be different . . . the purpose of his knowledge is to govern his *action*" (314). Gadamer works through an analogy between ethical action and hermeneutical action which I believe can be extended beyond its structural similarities: both courses of interpretive and ethical action involve the notion of obligation, in that the situation, ethical or textual, itself demands to be read, demands a response to "the moment" (322). As ethical action is guided by application to the moment, so too is interpretive action: "The interpreter seeks no more than to understand this universal, the text—that is, to understand what it says, what constitutes the text's meaning and significance. In order to understand that, he must not try to disregard himself and his particular hermeneutical situation. He must relate the text to this situation if he wants to understand at all" (324). The point Gadamer makes about *phronesis* adapting itself to the moment can be extended into the sense that the understanding of text—as moment or "event"—is articulated precisely within a "dialogue" unique to a specific historical temporality: the hermeneutic situation must to a degree facilitate and dictate the means of its own particular reading. It is here that we can begin to unravel the implications of Beckett's "obligation." The hermeneutical response to Beckett is, as I will posit, an ethical response in that it articulates itself within a continuing critical dialogue, both with preceding criticism and with the reader's ongoing "self-conscious" metahermeneutic: the affective power of the Beckett text obliges continual response. It is the responsibility of the critic to make sense of the semiological-philosophical contexts from which and to which this response orients itself. The Beckettian reading subject, whose readings always appear "merely" as readings and hence whose meaning status is provisional, is not thus one I wish to figure as mere product or producer of words "with no ground for their settling." I disagree, therefore, with some deconstructive readings of Beckett that claim Beckett has effected, as Ileana Marculescu claims in her essay "Beckett and the Temptation of Solipsism," a "systematic deconstruction of language and of meaning" (55). Although I am comfortable with placing a provisionality within the hermeneutical conversation, I wish to emphasize that an ethical reading of Beckett, though not final, is, as *active* reading orienting itself to a particular semiological instant, nevertheless always potentially "meaningful."

The reader and character thus occupy similar ontological positions with regard to their hermeneutical apprehensions of this (narrative) world. Understanding the philosophical implications of this relationship (I use the term "specular" to account for the manner in which the reader's hermeneutic dilemma is mirrored by that of the character) is another of the reader's obligations to the Beckett text. This aspect of my project is not simply an application of Gadamer to Beckett: it is an exploration of the interpenetration of Gadamerian, or, more precisely, Aristotelian ethics and Beckett's character's own articulated sense of "obligation" to express, which I suggest has as concomitant an obligation to interpret. If, as the narrator of *The Unnamable* puts it, "I am obliged to speak," the reader has an immediate responsibility to make sense of that obligatory locution; indeed, given the specular relation between character and reader, the reader has no choice but to make sense of all discursive acts in the texts because, in a very real sense, the acts of the character become the acts of the reader. This obligation, this ethic, not only configures the reading experience as one of endless textuality but introduces an element of responsibility into the dynamic. This element problematizes a strictly postmodern or poststructuralist reading of Beckett, as a system of ethics seems always to threaten to reconfigure the subject and, therefore, to reconfigure a basic metaphysical premise of the ground of Being. Indeed, one of the questions I explore here is the possibility of ethics given the various ontologically suspect subjects and situations in Beckett's novels: Is ethics possible in a universe of pure discourse? Or, to give the question a slightly different slant, is a poststructuralist reading of Beckett entirely possible given that a ghost of ethics still haunts the narrators?

Interpreting Narrative in the Novels of Samuel Beckett is divided into six chapters (with an introduction and conclusion). Chapter 1, a reading of Beckett's *Watt*, explores the relation between the title character's failing language and the hermeneutic appropriation of this discourse by the reader. While Watt's language decomposes itself, the reader is met with the heightened awareness of the obligation to read what very well may be an unreadable discourse. In my reading of this novel (Beckett's final novel in English before the turn into French) I isolate several instances in which what I have termed the specular relation between reader and character is created. These instances all involve specific moments of reading; indeed, I figure this novel as an extended exploration of the hermeneutic act. Watt's acts of reading are *mise-en-abymes* of the larger act of reading undertaken by the reader of the novel itself, and because Watt's acts of reading ultimately "fail," the novel thematizes the impossibility of hermeneutics even as it makes the interpretive act a central fact of Being. This novel thus instantiates the general tenor of the hermeneutic dilemma in all the subsequent novels by figuring the act of reading as the act of a failing hermeneutic.

Chapter 2 continues the exploration of this aporia by suggesting an inexorable link between the narrative and hermeneutic gestures in *Mercier and Camier*, reading both as responses to specific mechanisms of desire for order, or what Paul Ricoeur calls "directedness." This novel, often dismissed by Beckettians as an "experiment," presents the reader with a narrative that replicates itself as it proceeds. After every second chapter of *Mercier and Camier,* the narrative stops and the preceding action is summarized. I figure these summaries as emblems of a desire for this directedness, as instances in which the narrative becomes aware of the need for hermeneutic stability: indeed, these chapter summaries are the novel's own reading of itself. *Mercier and Camier* therefore collapses any possible epistemological differences between the act of narration and the act of interpretation. This collapsing, moreover, is prefigured in the narrative's distrust of its own first premises as narrative; the summaries, more than interpretive acts, are implicit reminders that the act of narration can never itself fully succeed in communicating experience. In Beckett a supplement to the act of narration is always needed and is built into the fabric of the narrative act. Thus to attempt any hermeneutic of this novel is to engage in an act anticipated and figured as futile by *Mercier and Camier* itself.

Chapter 3 analyzes Gadamer's articulation of the "dialogical" function in hermeneutics as it relates to *Molloy* to suggest that the paradox of the Beckettian narrator arises as the speaking/narrating subject fractures itself into what Beckett calls "the impossible voice," that purely discursive position of hallucinating the ontological reality of the self-as-simulacrum. *Molloy* is a narrative that parodies the epistemological presuppositions of the detective or police procedural. In this genre the logic of pursuit is simply taken for granted in such a manner as to suppose that the basic epistemological opposition of subject and object obtains. As Molloy is pursued by Moran it begins to become clear that any ontological separation between subject (Moran) and object (Molloy) cannot be maintained; indeed, one of the themes of the novel is the notion that self can never be separated from Other, that subject always adheres to (or adheres "in") object. As it parodies the basic premises of the detective procedural, *Molloy* also interrogates the grounds of a Gadamerian hermeneutics by calling into question—or at least reconfiguring—what it means to engage in a hermeneutical dialogue. I suggest that *Molloy* registers a profound distrust of the ability of the self to engage the world in interpretive dialogue precisely by challenging the epistemological grounds of a philosophical hermeneutics, that of the comfortable separation of subject and object.

Chapter 4 tightens the focus on these general hermeneutic themes. In my reading of *Malone Dies* I draw on the theories of Gadamer, Ricoeur, and Huizinga to explore the hermeneutical function of "play" in the novel. Play is a hugely important theme in philosophical hermeneutics. Both Gadamer and Ricoeur figure the moment of hermeneutics, the moment in which the subject enters the interpretive conversation with the text (person, tradition), as a moment of play, as, precisely, a moment in which the subject loses a sense of self. Play, and ultimately hermeneutics, can succeed only if the player (hermeneut) loses him or herself and undergoes some form of transfiguration in contact with the text at hand. Without this giving up of self, and the concomitant transfiguration, the hermeneutic act will fail. Ultimately, the suggestion in my analysis of *Malone Dies* is that the stories told by Malone over the course of his narrative, a process he calls "play" ("I am going to play" [180]), can succeed narratologically and hermeneutically only if the speaking subject loses an awareness of self, if the narrating subject can successfully imitate that moment of absolute nonbeing, or death. Malone is telling stories to fill the time until his death, and the stories he tells, in which he attempts, but fails, to lose himself, act as rehearsals for the ultimate moment of the loss of self in death. Malone, however, like all Beckett narrators, is extraordinarily self-conscious, consistently recalling himself to himself as the narrative proceeds: "What tedium. And I call that playing" (189). The aporia for Malone is that his stories will fail precisely because they cannot call into being that moment of utter dissolution so feared and desired by the Beckettian narrator. In fact, *Malone Dies* is founded on what I call the logic of paradox. Malone is attempting to inscribe the moment of death, the moment of absolute nonbeing (or, indeed, the moment of "absolute play"). This attempt is of course logically impossible. Only a silence in the *end* of writing will bring about this moment, a silence the Beckett narrator is never to achieve.

Chapter 5 discusses *The Unnamable* as a self-interpreting, or what I call "metahermeneutic," system that reads—or attempts to read—itself through the definitional and ethical thresholds of beginning, ending, and obligation. This chapter is an attempt to give a specifically ethical reading of *The Unnamable,* to suggest how the Unnamable's "obligation" to speak is more than logorrhoeic compulsion but is in fact an index of a profound sense of the responsibilities and power of (Being in) discourse. The responsibility of the reader of this text is to gauge the philosophical, hermeneutic, and semiotic resonance of "obligation" as it maps onto the Unnamable's narrative, to gauge, more problematically, how the thematics of ethical obligation is manifested in a semiology—more specifically an *aesthetic* semiology—without firm discursive or subjective boundaries. The Unnamable's narrative at once draws on "traditional" ethics and dismantles the very logic of such an ethical economy by figuring the narrating subject as "beyond" such categories as "beginning" and "ending" and thus as a subject impossible to locate. Thus the question of prime importance in *The Unnamable* is that of the logic of ethics (as obligation) under the constraints of a radically fragmented subjectivity: Whence obligation for a decentered subject? The question becomes more complicated when we gauge the resonance of the fact that the Unnamable's universe is constructed entirely of words, of discourse: "the end, the beginning, the beginning again, how can I say it, that's all words, they're all I have" (413). Can the ethical moment be a moment of pure discourse? Ultimately, my suggestion here is that ethics, as an orienting response to the vagaries and variabilities of Being, is precisely a fact or result of being-in-language. As the subject inhabits the world through and within language, ethics becomes inseparable from the hermeneutic act as the act of interpretation always orients itself to polysemous contexts. The logic of this formulation, and the logic of *The Unnamable,* suggests that any situation is potentially interpretable and hence demanding of ethical response: the very fact of being-in-the-world is *necessarily* ethical.

Chapter 6 explores the relation between memory, desire, suffering, and death and the constitution of the narrating subject in *How It Is* and theorizes the implications of Being in the discursive space of repetition. In this pivotal text Beckett moves from thematizing a particular hermeneutic problem to a more generalized thematization of the hermeneutics of Being. The fundamental question this text explores is that of the hermeneutic subject articulated in a general economy of suffering. But because *How It Is* represents itself as an extended quotation ("how it was I quote" [7]), it immediately configures and articulates itself in the discursive space of repetition, and thus the entire problematic of the representation of repetition anticipates the difficulty of locating the present moment of Being and, more precisely, the present moment of suffering in the narrator's story. What is at stake in this text of "midget grammar" (76) is the efficacy of representation, the representation of the fact of suffering in the discursive and ethical space of repetition, the space, to borrow from Heidegger's *Being and Time,* of "having-been." The crucial question in *How It Is* is narratological and thus ultimately hermeneutical: *When* is suffering? I read this novel through a matrix of converging hermeneutic lenses (including the work of Heidegger, Blanchot, Deleuze, Baudrillard, and Benjamin), all of which touch upon or use as a point of departure this notion of the (a)temporality of suffering. I thus theorize a conceptual space within which to read Beckett's narrating subject, a subject who moves inexorably toward death but who simultaneously articulates itself in extended quotation ("A word from me and I am again"): Beckett's subject thus delimits the space of death by suggesting that to die is merely to die again.

My concluding chapter attempts to point the way to a fruitful hermeneutical analysis of Beckett's drama and later prose (*Endgame, Company, Ill Seen Ill Said, Worstward Ho*). If there is an overarching hermeneutic theme in all of Beckett's texts, it would be that of the dialogical function, that function vital to the scene of (self-)interpretation. Each text, whether in its particular textual economy or as it obliges the hermeneutic reader, articulates the dialogical principle if only to dismantle it. Fixing the subjectivity of the hermeneutic speaker of the Beckett text, that subjectivity fundamentally dependent on establishing itself in (aporetic) dialogue, thus proves ultimately impossible because the voice of the subject is itself "impossible." I am intrigued by the possibilities of a hermeneutical analysis of Beckett's later prose, primarily because these are texts that have rewritten the ground rules of genre and in turn begun to construct a language that has, I think, made it difficult even to formulate the beginning of a hermeneutical stance from which to apprehend the texts. In short, I think we have yet fully to understand what these texts are, and before we do, we cannot move very far into them. I am convinced that one way into these texts is through the lens of dialogue because, in understanding how dialogue operates to articulate the subject, to frame the basic structure of how the hermeneutical conversation is thematized and actualized in the reader of the text, we take a step toward understanding the basic conditions or grounds for formulating the possibility of reading.

This problematic of aporetic dialogue is continually thematized in Beckett's later texts, including the second trilogy, *Ill Seen Ill Said, Worstward Ho, Company,* and the drama. In this final chapter I take as a test case Beckett's 1957 drama *Endgame*. As a drama, *Endgame* articulates itself in a different semiotic context than the novels, but Beckett's profound concern with the dialogical principle still remains and, indeed, is that much more important given that drama is a medium that traditionally privileges dialogue above all else. I suggest that *Endgame* is an elaborate exploration of the absence of the dialogical function. There is of course dialogue in the play in the mundane sense of the word—and it is dialogue, as Hamm suggests, that keeps Clov "here" (58)—but as Clov also rightly suggests, the words making up that discourse may no longer have any meaning: "I use the words you taught me. If they don't mean anything any more, teach me others. Or let me be silent" (44). Without a constitutive language, "world" cannot be disclosed, dialogue cannot be grounded or even posited. My analysis of the second trilogy is grounded in the idea that the narrating subject is divided between temporalities, between states of being. As a result of this division, the subject is a priori thrust into a dialogical position of listening to the self, speaking to the self, devising the self as at once present and non-self-coincidental. The profound irony of the Beckettian text as it is read through the hermeneutical lens of this dialogic function is that the subject is articulated into a zone that compels dialogue even as it denies its hermeneutic viability. The result of this aporetic dialogical matrix is the ever-retreating narrator, the narrative voice endlessly impossible to locate. Yet, as I observe finally, all narrators are located within a self-conscious language: language still functions even if only as a gauge of its own impossibility. These later texts retrace the fact of Being in language that is explored in the earlier novels: the fact of Being in language that at once composes and decomposes the subject, the fact of Being in a language whose end is never to be but exists, to quote from *Worstward Ho*, at the paradoxical "bounds of a boundless void" (47), the fact of Being in an impossibility but still in a language that articulates its impossibility in what Beckett calls the "nohow on."

I

Watt

> This fragility of the outer meaning had a bad effect on Watt, for it caused him to seek for another, for some meaning of what had passed, in the image of how it passed.
> —*Watt*

Samuel Beckett's *Watt* is commonly acknowledged in the corpus of Beckett criticism as signaling a departure from the heady precocity and slightly jejune indulgence of *Murphy*. Some notable exceptions aside, the text is generally categorized and framed somewhat dismissively as an "experiment," one with new discourses, philosophies, and ideologies. The text is, moreover, understood as being in some ways a mere preamble or prologue to the trilogy and, as such, does not receive the specific hermeneutic treatment it deserves. Rather than accepting this interpretive current, I suggest that *Watt* is Beckett's crucial turn into a fully "hermeneutic" mode of writing, one that thematizes, and ultimately parodies, the problematics of interpretation even as it offers itself as interpretable object. *Watt* has as a central concern the struggle with language and the essential linguistic nature of experience. Language in this pivotal work acts as a barrier to any "fullness" of understanding: disclosure of meaning is, therefore, either deferred or acknowledged through a variety of strategies to be a priori unavailable.[1] Nevertheless, the pursuit of meaning begins because the obligation framing that pursuit cannot, or will not, be elided even under despair or acknowledged absurdity. A hermeneutic reading of Watt's reading of his world (one mode of what I call the metahermeneutic gesture) acknowledges the degree to which he expresses, however oddly, the force of a desire: desire and hermeneutics, *Watt* suggests, are the two faces of the same coin.

A hermeneutic reading of *Watt* is as complex as the plot of the novel itself is simple: Watt, for unknown reasons, makes a journey to a house owned and inhabited by a Mr. Knott; Watt enters into the service of Knott; Watt replaces an outgoing servant just as he will be replaced when he leaves; Watt eventually works his way up from the basement to the first floor to attend personally on Knott; Watt begins to experience what appears to be a mental collapse after beginning to perceive that Knott's "world" seems not to correspond to generally held notions of "reality"; Watt leaves Knott's house. During his residence at Knott's establishment, Watt begins to communicate in increasingly bizarre ways (for example, speaking backward): his spoken discourse thus begins to reflect the peculiar "ontology" of Knott's world.

It has been generally accepted that Watt's residence at Knott's establishment is the cause of his radical mental/linguistic collapse. This observation, however, has not led to any full interrogation either of the rhetorical structures of this discourse of "madness" or of the effect on the reader of Watt's increasingly bizarre language. It has not been fully appreciated that, regardless of the "fact" that Watt is losing rational control, the reader is constrained by the boundaries of the text to attempt to make sense of his experience. The ideas I will explore here build on Roland Barthes's comment in his "Introduction to the Structural Analysis of Narratives" that in a text "everything has a meaning or nothing has" (104): the discourse of madness is still a discourse and, moreover, as it is "framed" by narrative, demands to be read. Barthes points out that our reactions to any fictionalized discourse are determined by the context of that discourse. The narrative object contains elements *meaning* to be read: it thus confers an obligation on its reader. In this sense, to label Watt a madman is useful, if at all, only as a description, since we must make use of his language as we attempt to make "sense" of it.

My interest here is, ultimately, to explore Beckett's manipulation of the "meaning to be read" aspect of this text. Beckett consistently interrogates the boundaries of the readable to the point that every interpretation of his work is compelled to question the entire notion *of* the aesthetic and thus the hermeneutical apprehension of the aesthetic object. This process of challenging interpretive boundaries with its concomitant thematization of reading and reader begins with *Watt:* I see the text thus as an extended allegory or parable of reading, an announcement by Beckett of a shift into a writing that theorizes itself as hermeneutic object as it proceeds. In my analysis Watt will stand as an emblem of the reader and of the process of reading itself.[2] Both Watt and reader begin, but perhaps do not end, in a similar posture of ignorance. Framed as such, my reading moves away from attempting to ascertain "meaning" to one that continually shifts from a reading of specific scenes of interpretation to my own theorizing of the reader's encounter with those scenes of reading.³ The process of "reading through reading"—a process I call metahermeneutics—ultimately places the reader in specular relation to Watt, ultimately compels the reader to balance his or her hermeneutic desire against the exigencies of Watt's own interpretive praxis. More concretely, in this chapter I attempt to account in hermeneutic terms for the anxiety produced in the reading of this text, anxiety that arises in the reader's own self-conscious awareness of his or her proximity to the radical "otherness" of Watt, the parodic hermeneut.

My use of the term "specular" here draws from two traditions in the human sciences. The first is the late phenomenological tradition of Gadamer, Ricoeur, Wolfgang Iser, and Hans Jauss. In this hermeneutic tradition a central place is given to the self-conscious reader, one who is aware that his or her identity *as* reader is formed in intimate relation to the text. The text in some ways functions as a mirror reflecting back what the reader brings to the reading experience, much as a mirror reflects the image of the viewer. My metaphor of specularity is an attempt to relate the phenomenological tradition of *self*-awareness to the experience of reading texts that in some ways deny the very grounds of self. As readers move through Beckett's corpus they finds themselves in increasingly close relation to the experience of the characters in the novel: their hermeneutic bafflement mirrors or is mirrored by the character's own; their experience of what Heidegger calls "thrownness" is identical to that of the character;⁴ their sense of the necessity to read is close to that of the character. The hermeneutic tradition is founded on the idea that reading subject and read object must maintain separate but related autonomies, that readers are not to lose themselves in the reading experience but in some sense bring themselves to the text in order to find, to see, themselves. In *Truth and Method* Gadamer puts it thus:

> A person trying to understand a text is prepared for it to tell him something. That is why a hermeneutically trained consciousness must be, from the start, sensitive to the text's alterity. But this kind of sensitivity involves neither "neutrality" with respect to content nor the extinction of one's self, but the foregrounding and appropriation of one's own fore-meanings and prejudices. (269)⁵

Ricoeur brings the issue of hermeneutic specularity to the foreground in his essay "What Is a Text?" He writes, "What the interpreter says is a re-saying which reactivates what is said in the text" (164). This reawakening, as Gadamer insists, always involves the reader's self-evaluation: the text reflects the self to the self. Ricoeur discusses his crucial notion of "appropriation":

> By "appropriation" I understand this: that the interpretation of a text culminates in the self-interpretation of a subject who thenceforth understands himself better, understands himself differently, or simply begins to understand himself.... On the one hand, understanding the text is not an end in itself... *in hermeneutic reflection—or in reflective hermeneutics—the constitution of the self is contemporaneous with the constitution of meaning.* (158–59; emphasis added)

It is precisely here—in this matrix of meaning formation and self-formation—that my term "specularity" is intended to be of most use. Reading Beckett, I suggest, is not merely about attempting to fix the meaning of the text; it is always a process of coming to an understanding of one's self in relation to a text that resists meaning. The reader's desire in relation to the Beckett text thus is double: a desire for meaning constituted *as* a desire for self-understanding.

While my theoretical focus here is primarily that of the phenomenological-hermeneutical tradition, I am of course also drawing on Jacques Lacan's seminal discussion of ego formation in his "The Mirror Stage as Formative of the Function of the I" as I touch on this issue of specularity. It is not my intention to give a psychoanalytical reading of Beckett but I do intend to examine how the reading of Beckett's texts conflates a series of *desires*. I will suggest that Beckett's texts foreground the intimate conjunction of interpretive and what I call "subjective" desires: that is, the experience of the text is one of coming to realize the degree to which the formation of the reading self—the competency of the reading self—is bound to a recognition of the self within the text. Lacan argues that the formation of the ego is based on a primal identification, a recognition of the self as he or she assumes an image. Lacan's argument is quite close to that of Ricoeur; both see the formation of the self as one of transformation-as-identification. Ricoeur sees the self as "conferred by the work itself" ("Appropriation"). Lacan writes: "We have only to understand the mirror stage *as an identification,* in the full sense that analysis gives to the term: namely, the transformation that takes place in the subject when he assumes an image—whose predestination to this phase-effect is sufficiently indicated by the use, in analytic theory of the ancient term *imago*" (2). Lacan concludes his essay with the suggestion that the formation of ego is based not on totalizing recognitions—that is, that the self is formed as a whole through a totalized act of seeing—but that the self is predicated on the "*function of méconnaissance* [misrecognition]" (6). I am intrigued by the possibilities of a hermeneutics of misrecognition, by the idea that the reading self in Beckett is formed in a process of what Beckett calls "ill-seeing." Lacan thus provides a counterpoint to the hermeneutic tradition that, it sometimes seems, credits the reader with overmuch interpretive power and agency.

A reading of the history of the critical reception of Beckett's *Watt* demonstrates the degree to which this protean, enigmatic, and interrogative text seems consistently to demand a reading that puts an end to the text's potentially endless play of signifiers. There is an almost universal acknowledgment that the text is concerned with matters of language but an equally universal failure to acknowledge the manner in which the text implicates, seduces, and obliges the reader's own hermeneutic discourse. *Watt* is an extraordinarily difficult text to read: to enter fully Watt's world means, as I suggest here, to come into close contact with a mind in absolute crisis. Such an experience is the cause of anxiety in some critics, whose readings of *Watt* demonstrate ultimately a desire for a comfortable interpretive distance from this altogether disconcerting work.

Michael Robinson's *Long Sonata of the Dead* acknowledges *Watt* as "the opening encounter with the disturbing meaning of the imponderables that have occupied [Beckett] ever since" (101). He frames Watt as a rationalist (a common enough gesture) confronted by the void attempting desperately to define his situation. Robinson makes a connection between Watt's increasing "madness" and the "collapse" of language: "As a rationalist faced with the inexplicable, Watt resorts to the enumeration of every logical possibility implicit in a given situation, hoping to find in the sum of all the data a permutation of the facts that will include the correct assumption and so set his mind at rest" (105). At the end of his analysis, Robinson frames Watt as a humanized clown or Christ figure in an allegorical gesture symptomatic of the need to "end" the play of the text.

H. Porter Abbott also suggests that Watt's difficulties stem from the inability to secure meaning in an aleatory universe. Abbott makes the leap beyond the text to suggest, valuably, the homology between Watt and the reader. His analysis, however, is carefully qualified as if he is fearful of the full implications of his own idea of "imitative form": "I am not claiming the reader's experience is precisely that of Watt, nor that through it he comprehends the ineffability of all things and experience. But the point is that the form . . . is used to generate in the reader an experience approaching the experience that is its 'content'" (61). Abbott's analysis falls short of fully interrogating the inevitable implications of what he calls imitative form. Though he moves to acknowledge the reader through Watt-as-emblem, he seems content to delineate the "form" of the relationship between text and reader. Abbott concludes his analysis of *Watt* in a manner remarkably similar to that of Robinson. He maps out an allegorical, archetypal reading of the text, positing *Watt*, finally, as a kind of anti-romance.

Angela Moorjani's complex analysis in *Abysmal Games in the Novels of Samuel Beckett* outlines the form and theme of the text: "Thematically the novel's embedded games can be linked to a retrospective testing of the philosophical categories that through the ages have been applied to the human condition" (84); she sees the novel dismantling "the monuments of Western thought" (84)—an onerous task indeed.

The point I wish to emphasize here is the degree to which readings of this text concentrate merely on the text, fail to give adequate attention to the philosophical implications of hermeneutics (including Watt's own), and merely, through varying degrees of complexity, trace the outline, shape, or form of the novel without interrogating either the gesture itself or the fact that the novel seems readable only through this tracing. The novel often reduces the critic to extremely local or discrete biographical or allegorical readings; hence John P. Harrington's attempt to stabilize *Watt* through a reading of its Irish geography ("The Irish Landscape of Samuel Beckett's *Watt*"); Gottfried Buttner's bizarre reading of *Watt* as an extended intrauterine fantasy (*Samuel Beckett's Novel Watt*); Leslie Hill's emphasis on Knott as an elusive, elided father figure whose absence provokes the dispersal of meaning (*Beckett's Fiction: In Different Words*); and David H. Hesla, who in *The Shape of Chaos* writes: "Watt's journey to Knott's house is a fairly close parallel with the stations of the cross" (62).

These critics employ a hermeneutics of cessation. If they acknowledge that their readings are provisional, there is still a sense in which the insidious play of the text, by being framed, for instance, in allegory, has ceased or has been stilled. A reading of the importance of reading in the text might in turn be questioned as being yet another allegorical framework—*Watt* being "about" the reader's relationship to *Watt* as text. I will argue that reading *as* hermeneutic reading—a reading conferred by Beckett's text itself—is never, and can never be, a stilling of text precisely because it theorizes reading as continual obligatory "event": a hermeneutic reading thus is fundamentally processual, fundamentally dynamic, as it orients itself from and to various scenes of interpretation. A hermeneutic interpretation will acknowledge that there is no finality to any reading; judgments are made in relation to discrete events in texts, and thus any work cannot be reduced to any totalizing allegory.

A hermeneutic reading finally acknowledges textuality so as to effect a precarious balance between constraints of discrete textual event and the larger, and in the case of *Watt*, protean, processual whole. In the following analysis I trace Watt's own hermeneutic process through three discrete interpretive scenes in order to suggest several things. First, by reading the specific modes of Watt's interpretive practice against some specifics of Gadamerian theory, I wish to trace the development of Watt's own hermeneutic, from its initial articulation as a kind of aporetic allegory, to its final status as a resigned acquiescence to the unreadable, the Unnamable.[6] I will suggest, ultimately, that Watt's interpretive anxiety stems as much from a refusal to follow through on his own hermeneutic insights as from any congenital difficulties he may have. Second, I am concerned with touching briefly on the implications of Gadamer's notion of understanding as "dialogue" and "appropriation," as outlined in his essay "On the Problem of Self-Understanding" and in *Truth and Method*. He suggests that understanding occurs only as the interpreter makes his or her own the discourse of that which he or she attempts to understand. I suggest that Beckett heightens our awareness of understanding as appropriation through his manipulation of Watt. Beckett compels readers—in a process I call "conferred appropriation"—to make their own a discourse of baffling and deliberate complexity by compelling them literally to translate Watt's increasingly bizarre and already specular language and ultimately to act, in Derrida's sense of the term, as a kind of hermeneutic "supplement" to Watt's refusal of hermeneutics, his "anterior default of a presence" (*Of Grammatology* 145). Reading Beckett is as much about the process of reading itself as it is about making specific interpretations of the meaning of the work. Indeed, I hope this chapter will serve as a step toward understanding the logic of a text that paradoxically "denies" the logic of interpretation by inscribing—and parodying—its own reading *en abyme:* "But what was this pursuit of meaning, in this indifference to meaning? And to what did it tend? These are delicate questions" (72).

The initial and initiatory act of reading in *Watt* is Watt's attempt to frame the incident with the piano-tuning Galls within a consistent metastructure, that is, within a frame that makes sense of the structure of the Galls' mutterings. The Galls, father and son, have arrived at Knott's house to "choon" the piano. They engage in the following esoteric exchange:

> The mice have returned, he said.
> The elder said nothing. Watt wondered if he had heard.
> Nine dampers remain, said the younger, and an equal number of hammers.
> Not corresponding, I hope, said the elder.
> In one case, said the younger.
> The elder had nothing to say to this.
> The strings are in flitters, said the younger.
> The elder had nothing to say to this either.
> The piano is doomed, in my opinion, said the younger.
> The piano-tuner also, said the elder.
> The pianist also, said the younger.
> This was perhaps the principal incident of Watt's early days in Mr. Knott's house. (68–69)

This "principal incident" shares a homology with "all incidents of note proposed to Watt" (69) during his tenure with Knott. The incident of course is not precisely clear either to Watt or to his reader. What has occurred during this entirely linguistic exchange (if indeed "exchange" is the word)? It is an incident the semantics, if not semiotics, of which give way in Watt to an emotional response to, or desire for, form: "For the incident of the Galls father and son was followed by others of a similar kind, incidents that is to say of great formal brilliance and indeterminable purport" (71). Any potential meaning is elided as the hermeneutic begins:

> It resembled them ["all incidents of note"] in the sense that it was not ended when it was past, but continued to unfold, in Watt's head, from beginning to end, over and over again, the complex connexions of its lights and shadows, the passing from silence to sound and from sound to silence, the stillness before the movement and the stillness after, the quickenings and retardings, the approaches and the separations, all the shifting detail of its march and ordinance, according to the irrevocable caprice of its taking place. It resembled them in the vigour with which it developed a purely plastic content, and gradually lost, in the nice processes of its light, its sound, its impacts and its rhythm, all meaning, even the most literal. (69)

This is for Watt an initiation into the hermeneutic (of the void). Watt, the man who "had not seen a symbol, nor executed an interpretation, since the age of fourteen, or fifteen" (70), and who had lived among "face values" (70) until now, has stepped precariously into a reading of a kind of deep structure. Here "face value"—the incident, if we can even locate the incident—is elided figurally into shape in a conscious process of substitution. This process originates with Watt's complete inability to maintain the crucial relation between surface (face) and depth as he reads various incidents. Each element of any reading acts as counterbalance to the other; to lose sight of the surface meaning (or affect) of a given word, theme, or symbol is to plunge headlong into a form of allegory that has as its final effect a complete inability to orient the reading to the "real" from which the reader must orient *himself*: this process of ill-reading defines Watt's predicament here precisely. Hermeneutics for Watt takes the form of an expression of a desire for mastery over the given event (text), a mastery that removes the event from a context of potential meaningfulness to one in which the reader frames the event from a position of supremacy: any dialogical interplay between text/event and reader is suppressed in Watt.

I here emphasize a particular dynamic of Watt's early reading that few critics care to notice. Most are comfortable suggesting simply that meaning is unavailable to Watt because of a congenital difficulty or philosophical bent (but perhaps they are one and the same?). Few care to notice the *mode* of his reading in its particular hermeneutical context:

> And Watt could not accept them [the series of similar incidents] for what they perhaps were, the simple games that time plays with space, now with these toys, and now with these, *but was obliged*, because of his peculiar character to enquire into what they meant, oh not into what they really meant, his character was not so peculiar as all that, but into what they might be *induced to mean*, with the help of a little patience, a little ingenuity. (71–72; emphasis added)

Watt, as indicated in the epigraph to this chapter, does not seek an understanding of the event; he refuses to allow the event to speak its meaning to him. Rather he engages in a species of reading by deferral, or reading by simulacrum: he seeks for some meaning of what had passed, "in the image of how it passed" (70). This particular mode of reading is predicated in the void: where the particular instance has no particular image, to make sense of it necessarily, it seems, means that one has to speak of it in other images. The narrator defines this hermeneutics of deferral:

> For the only way one can speak of nothing is to speak of it as though it were something, just as the only way one can speak of God is to

speak of him as though he were a man, which to be sure he was, in a sense, for a time, and as the only way one can speak of man, even our anthropologists have realized that, is to speak of him as though he were a termite. (74)

The aporia, for the reader as for Watt, begins with the narrator's delicate qualification of Watt's success in reading the Galls incident: "But if Watt was sometimes unsuccessful, and sometimes successful, as in the affair of the Galls father and son, in foisting a meaning there where no meaning appeared, he was most often neither the one, nor the other" (74). Watt is neither successful nor unsuccessful, neither the one nor the other. Beckett presents a (negative?) binary here the interplay of which defines Watt's—and our—predicament precisely. It seems rather uncomfortable though perhaps inevitable to assume that as Watt is neither successful nor unsuccessful he lies somewhere in the middling range of success. But is this a correct gauging of the choice? It seems rather more likely that any rigidly logical reading of this ("he was more often neither the one, nor the other") leaves us nowhere at all. Beckett opens up, as Paul Davies suggests in *The Ideal Real*, a new "ontology" in which the logical constraints of and on the linguistic fall away or apart into a new sensibility, neither rational, irrational, logical, nor absurd. We are in a precarious no-man's-land in our readings of Beckett's characters' reading where a vertiginous blurring of sense into nonsense, or nonsense into sense, defines our reading posture.

I have suggested here that one response to this new ontology is to engage in a species of reading that this text, as far as I can gather, would seem neither to condemn nor to praise but slowly to dismantle. The critical mania for allegory is, I think, subtly parodied here by Beckett, who suggests that to substitute something for nothing (*allegoria:* "other speaking"), no matter the desire for what the narrator will call "semantic succour" (79) and no matter the comfort it may bring, is still to substitute something for *nothing*. To begin to read correctly Beckett's "nothing" means that we have to reframe it affectively. I think most critics accept that Beckett's texts are "nothing" in substance, the most famous formulation of this idea being Vivian Mercier's categorization of *Godot* as the play in which nothing happens, twice. Nothing of "substance" may occur in Beckett, but affectively these texts have volumes of occurrence, and it is in and out of a thematization of this affective response to "nothing" that our readings must begin.[7]

And it is affectively out of "nothing" that our reading of Watt's reading appears. We are constrained to follow his laborious, and somewhat disconcerting, descent into interpretation; his interpretive acts, however, seem never to orient themselves to anything tangible. It is the peculiar nature of this text that our tracings of Watt's reading are always already tracings of tracings. Moreover, our interpretations tend not toward events themselves but toward interpretations of interpretations of nebulous events: the event in *Watt* is continually receding temporally. Beckett signals this temporal slippage with his use of the deictic "now":

> But generally speaking it seems probable that the meaning attributed to this particular type of incident, by Watt, in his relations, was now the initial meaning that had been lost and then recovered, and now a meaning quite distinct from the initial meaning, and now a meaning evolved, after a delay of varying length, and with greater or less pains, from the initial absence of meaning. (76)

The narrator's discourse here has at least a double effect; as metainterpretation (precisely: an interpretation of Watt's account of interpretation to the belatedly identified narrator "Sam") the initial incident is at least at a second remove. As such, "interpretation" here will involve the idea that temporal distancing of an event will occur even as the event is recounted. These ideas turn on the word "now," which seems to exist here in at least two or three distinct temporalities: Watt's at the time of the original incident; the narrator's at the time of this re(ac)counting; ours at the time of our reading. The fabric of the textual recounting of this event itself points—as deixis—to the difficulties of locating the events temporally. The event, as it is framed, slips beyond the reach of the narrator's rhetoric. Again, we are in an aporetic moment here as we trace the processual nature of meaning formation in *Watt*: it is, moreover, a moment doubly aporetic as we remember, as we always must, that the original (or "initial") meaning was never defined precisely.

I have spent a great deal of time with the Galls incident because it is the initiatory act of reading in *Watt* for Watt and the reader. More important, perhaps, is the degree of specific theorizing of reading that surrounds the scene itself (the theorizing of Sam, who may be "translating" Watt's interpretation of his formal [non]interpretation). This incident is thus vital as it theorizes itself as interpretation at the moment of its articulation; the narrator's theory of aporetic allegory sees the merging of hermeneutic theory and practice. Moreover, by suggesting that these scenes of reading be read *en abyme* I am acknowledging how often the implications of Beckett's parody of allegory are passed over in the critical reception of this text: the Galls incident is at once a *mise-en-abyme* of the hermeneutics of the entire novel and an anticipation of the critical reception of the text. Beckett perfectly represents in Watt the anxiety of the critic who when confronted with disjunctive form must frame that form in different terms, allegorically. There is thus a certain irony in those readings that see Watt, the character, as a Christ figure or an elided father figure, or the novel as an extended intrauterine fantasy or a dismantling of the categories of Western thought. I am proposing here that an alternate reading is to see the text as an allegory of *reading,* for to do so is to acknowledge how the text activates the reader's own self-consciousness as it focuses attention on the (hermeneutic) substance of the text itself.

The second scene of reading informed by the specific problematics of (meta)interpretation is Watt's reading, or more precisely, the narrator's description of Watt's reading, of the painting of the fractured circle. This scene of reading compels the reader of *Watt* into a qualitatively different interpretive posture because here the reader is confronted with Watt's reading without clear (meta)interpretation by the narrator: like the dot, freed from the circle in the painting, this reading floats independent of any constraining commentary. Theory is no longer inscribed within the scene of reading and thus we begin to sense a divergence between Watt and reader. The reader is aware of him or herself "as" Watt—in the sense that he or she too is making sense of the painting "through" Watt—but the scene begins to confer a new posture on the reader, who now must him or herself theorize Watt's readings rather than, strictly speaking, theorizing the narrator's (or Watt's) theorizing of Watt's reading. Both Watt and reader enter the novel from a position of some ignorance; the reader, however, accrues, or is reminded of, his or her activity as reader as the novel proceeds (Watt, as I will attempt to demonstrate, never gains any degree of real "self"-awareness).

Beckett's manipulation of the distance between specular reader (Watt) and actual reader is perhaps not as insidious as it will be in later texts, the trilogy, for instance. A crucial aspect of the relationship between specular reader and reader in the later texts is the identical interpretive posture each must assume; it is a posture, I suggest, of identical ignorance about the ontology of the textual world. In *Watt,* however, the reader is able to read Watt against the deficiencies of his interpretive praxis. We can see where Watt cannot. This divergence allows the reader a degree of comfortable separation from the specular reader, whose violation is, but is not, our own. The reader is thus only "incrementally" involved in *Watt* when tracing Watt's discourse: the mediating layers of metahermeneutic theory give way as the text proceeds to the reader's own increasing obligation to make sense of Watt's interpretive discourse. Given the previous theory and the sense that it is "missing" in the later scenes of reading, the reader moves in to fill in the schemata of Watt's interpretation but is always aware of the degrees of separation between him or herself and Watt.

The painting has been variously interpreted as a discrete emblem of the relationship between Watt and Knott, as Watt attempts to locate himself (as the separated "dot" in the painting) in the larger order of (Knott's) things. I wish to make sense of Watt's reading of the painting as an interpretation of affect as much as of form. At the moment of Watt's account of the painting, the reader, who receives an image of the painting only through him, begins his or her own interpretation and evaluation of Watt's reading. The painting is described thus:

> The only other object of note in Erskine's room was a picture, hanging on the wall, from a nail. A circle, obviously described by a compass, and broken at its lowest point, occupied the middle foreground, of this picture. Was it receding? Watt had that impression. In the eastern background appeared a point, or dot. The circumference was black. The point was blue, but blue! The rest was white. (126)

Watt's reading of the painting is as complex as it is plodding. It touches on a variety of modes of interpretation, from formal, "historiographic," to a kind of prosopopeia, to allegory that speaks as much to our own readings of this specific text as to Watt's attempt to reach any kind of "semantic succour" in the painting. Watt begins with a formal analysis of parts: "By what means the illusion of movement in space, and it almost seemed in time, was given, Watt could not say. But it was given" (127); he continues by reading the parts prosopopeically: "Watt wondered if they had sighted each other, or were blindly flying thus, harried by some force of merely mechanical mutual attraction, or the playthings of chance" (127) as if, perhaps, humanizing these abstractions would be to understand them better. Still anthropomorphizing, Watt begins a list of all the "logical" permutations of relations that concludes with one of Watt's few overt displays of emotion in the novel: "And at the thought that it was perhaps this, a circle and a centre not its centre in search of a centre and its circle respectively, in boundless space, in endless time, then Watt's eyes filled with tears that he could not stem, and they flowed down his fluted cheeks unchecked, in a steady flow, refreshing him greatly" (127). From this moment of expression Watt contemplates the picture at different angles to conclude that its original hanging position is superior. Watt moves to platitudinal conclusions on the "human condition" which I am tempted to read as an attack on humanist interpretations of art. Watt here calls upon the artist as the final arbiter of meaning in his nostalgia for origins. This is a supremely comical mockery of the "intentional fallacy":

> And the thought of the point slipping in from below at last, when it came home at last, or to its new home, and the thought of the breach open below perhaps for ever in vain, these thoughts, to please Watt as they did, required the breach to be below and nowhere else. It is by the nadir that we come, said Watt, and it is by the nadir that we go, whatever that means. And the artist must have felt something of this kind too, for the circle did not turn, as circles will, but sailed steadfast in its white skies, with the patient breach for ever below. (128)

Watt concludes that all things at the Knott establishment are part of a process; there is no fixity, no surety—only flux. Watt's conclusion here dovetails nicely with a hermeneutical analysis of text because a true hermeneutics emphasizes the processual nature of understanding, as it is a dialogical "fusion of horizons" (*Truth and Method* 388): the hermeneutic encounter is a dynamic, never fully closed "conversation" (the word is Gadamer's). Understanding is not fixed and rigid, but rather it evolves and builds upon a series of incremental steps, much like Watt's reading of the painting. Watt makes a judgment here regarding Knott that theoretically should lead to a degree of succor. Watt's readings of Knott and his establishment, however, do not end here. Unsatisfied with this particular hermeneutic judgment, Watt blunders logically on. I say "logically" because I read Watt's reading of Knott through the logic of the question that informs our reading of *Watt* as a whole (thus a question that encompasses Watt's own reading): How does one understand process (or the process of understanding *understanding* as process) without halting that process, without parceling out the process in a manner that ceases the forward movement of understanding? Watt is, if we follow the logic of Gadamer's reading of understanding as process and tracing (or appropriation), inevitably to disrupt the original movement of that event: to appropriate finally is to alter.

It is of course impossible to understand process without in some ways halting that process. Watt's difficulties begin ultimately when the logic of this understanding is not fully grasped. A hermeneutics involves the reader's intimate conjunction of interpreter and event (Watt and Knott):

for the interpreter to understand event or the discourse of event he or she must in some ways disclose (to) him or herself, when "translating" event/text into his or her own discourse, a gesture that will inevitably disrupt the structurality of event/text. The event, as Gadamer suggests, does not exist in splendid isolation: the reader must bring it to him or herself in self-understanding. In Watt's process of reading the painting—which is ultimately a reading of Knott—he never does violate Knott's discrete autonomy as "text," never does effect a balance between the separated part and the representational whole of *this* hermeneutical circle, the painting. Watt's problem is finally a problem of self-understanding; his refusal to place the specter of Knott in intimate relation to himself is ultimately a refusal of interpretation. Knott cannot, the text suggests, be understood sui generis.

The crux and capstone of hermeneutical difficulty—or, as I have posited, refusal—in *Watt* is, of course, the tangled Knott himself. I am aided by Watt's own characterization of his relationship with Knott in my reading of Watt's refusal to read Knott. Knott's need of Watt is the Other's ethical need of being witnessed: "For except, one, not to need, and, two, a witness to his not needing, Knott needed nothing, as far as Watt could see. . . . And Mr. Knott, needing nothing if not, one, not to need, and two, a witness to his not needing, of himself knew nothing. And so he needed to be witnessed. Not that he might know, no, but that he might not cease" (202). We must remember that it is Watt who articulates these ideas: he himself finds his "conjecture not entirely gratuitous" (202) and defines his responsibility to Knott in what can be read as ethical terms. The narrator asks, perhaps anticipating the reader's question: "What kind of witness was Watt?" (202):

> A needy witness, an imperfect witness.
> The better to witness, the worse to witness.
> That with his need he might witness its absence.
> That imperfect he might witness it ill.
> That Mr. Knott might never cease, but ever almost cease. (202–3)

Watt, by "witnessing" his text (Knott), keeps that text from ceasing. Watt is, however, called on to "witness" the unwitnessable for Knott is, as the narrator suggests (transcribing Watt's words), protean. Watt catches sight of Knott as he is framed in his "eastern" window:

> Add to this that the figure of which Watt sometimes caught a glimpse, in the vestibule, in the garden, was seldom the same figure,

from one glance to the next, but so various, as far as Watt could make out, in its corpulence, complexion, height and even hair, and of course in its way of moving and of not moving that Watt would never have supposed it was the same, if he had not known that it was Mr. Knott. (146)

Knott's figure is essentially polymorphous and polysemous: "For one day Mr. Knott would be tall, fat, pale and dark, and the next thin, small, flushed and fair, and the next sturdy, middle-sized, yellow and ginger, and the next small, fat, pale, and fair" (209). He sings in a voice equally capable in "all male registers" (208) in a language "either without meaning, or derived from an idiom with which Watt, a very fair linguist, had no acquaintance" (208): he speaks, finally, in a language "meaningless to Watt's ailing ears" (208).

Confronted by this radical "meaninglessness" (or radical polysemy), Watt refuses to attempt to make a "reading" of Knott. Even to suggest Knott's need of summer or winter clothing is, for Watt, "an anthropomorphic insolence" (202); he is, and surely the word "anthropomorphic" recalls this, unwilling to substitute "something" for the nothing of Knott ("For the only way one can speak of nothing is to speak of it as though it were something, just as the only way one can speak of God is to speak of him as though he were a man" [74]). This phrase casts the eye back to Watt's initial articulation of the process of anthropomorphization—the substitution of something for nothing—and demonstrates a development in Watt's "mode" of reading. Where earlier "to explain had always been to exorcise, for Watt" (74–75) and where his practice had been to "induce" to meaning ("with the help of a little patience, a little ingenuity" [72]) that which resisted meaning, here with Knott it seems the free play of the sign(s) is simply acquiesced to.

It might be argued that by refusing to witness, Watt, from the premises of his own "conjecture," will cause the death of Knott. And indeed, it is this framework of witnessing the unwitnessable that Watt refuses when he departs the services of Knott:

> Watt suffered neither from the presence of Mr. Knott, nor from his absence. When he was with him, he was content to be with him, and when he was away from him, he was content to be away from him. Never with relief, never with regret, did he leave him at night, or in the morning come to him again. . . . So that when the time came for Watt to depart, he walked to the gate with the utmost serenity. (207)

In my reading of Watt's (non)reading of Knott I am playing on two meanings of the word "witness." Watt is an imperfect "witness" in two senses. Although he does observe (witness) Knott, he eventually simply leaves the establishment, ceasing his witnessing of Knott (he being one of a long line of employee-witnesses). Second, by refusing to "tell" (witness) the full narrative of his experiences, Watt again fails in his witnessing. Watt's final comment on Knott thus is crucial and substantiates my idea that Watt's inability to make sense of Knott is at least in part a refusal to make a fully hermeneutic reading of him: "Other traits, other little ways, little ways of passing the little days, Watt remarked in Mr. Knott, and could have told if he had wished, if he had not been tired, so very tired, by all he had told already, tired of adding, tired of subtracting to and from the same old things the same old things" (212). Watt's expression here is similar to that expression (of "Beckett"?) in the Addenda to the novel: "The following precious and illuminating material should be carefully studied. Only fatigue and disgust prevented its incorporation" (247). Fatigue and perhaps disgust prevent Watt from telling fully what he has observed of Knott. The point I wish to suggest here is partly a reaction against prevailing readings of Watt which see him fundamentally as passive victim, either of the mysterious process of Knott's order of things or of his own mental incapacity. I posit that this text, if read carefully through hermeneutic lenses, suggests that Watt too plays a large role in his decline. I do not wish to suggest Beckett's condemnation of Watt (such extratextual musings seem almost perversely out of place) but only another avenue of making sense of Watt's encounter with Knott. Watt does not finally take responsibility for his own readings in the sense that he simply allows the free play of signifiers to take its toll.

Watt's experience with Knott is thus one of continual bafflement and puzzlement. This bafflement produces in him a discursive "reaction" to Knott that speaks more to a desire to retreat from Knott than to understand him. Watt begins to speak in a specialized language that, in my reading, accomplishes two things. Instead of "translating" Knott's discourse—a discourse that perhaps is beyond Watt's understanding—Watt turns himself discursively into an analogue of Knott by mirroring the linguistic confusion he hears in Knott's own language; Watt, in perceiving the utter non-self-coincidence of the Other (Knott), dismantles grammatical and syntactical "logic," thereby dismantling the articulating self. Sam details Watt's process of reordering language: Watt moves from inverting the order of words (162); to inverting the order of letters within inverted words (163); to inverting the order of sentences (164); to inverting the letters of words and the sentences (164); to inverting "no longer the order of the words in the sentence together with that of the letters in the word, but that of the words in the sentence together with that of the sentences in the period" (165); to inverting "no longer the order of the words in the sentence together with that of the sentences in the period, but that of the letters in the word together with that of the sentences in the period" (165). We arrive finally at this:

> Dis yb dis, nem owt. Yad la, tin fo trap. Skin, skin, skin. Od su did ned taw? On. Taw ot klat tonk? On. Tonk ot klat taw? On. Tonk ta kool taw? On. Taw ta kool tonk? Nilb, mun, mud. Tin fo trap, yad la. Nem owt, dis yb dis. (166)
> (Sid by sid, two men. Al day, part of nit. Dum, num, blin. Knot look at Wat? No. Watt look at Knot? No. Wat talk to Knot? No. Knot talk to Wat? No. Wat den did us do? Niks, niks, niks. Part of nit, al day? Two men, sid by sid.)

In examining Watt's specular discourse we have to consider the rhetorical effect of the exigencies of "translation" on the reader. In his essay "On the Problem of Self-Understanding" Gadamer notes that understanding can occur only when the discourse of the event/text is "translated" into the interpreter's own discourse. This is a moment initiated by what I have called "tracing":

> To understand a text is to come to understand oneself in a kind of dialogue. This contention is confirmed by the fact that the concrete dealing with a text yields understanding only when what is said in the text begins to find expression in the interpreter's own language.
> ... One must take up into himself what is said to him in such fashion that it speaks and finds an answer in the words of his own language. (Gadamer 57)

Gadamer articulates here a sense of the constraints of the text on the interpreter's understanding, an understanding that must initially concretize that text. Of interest to the reader of Beckett's *Watt*—if one takes seriously Gadamer's proposition regarding understanding—is the manner in which the text imposes and impresses itself on its reader and thus attempts to forge a link, to use Levinas's terminology from *Totality and Infinity*, between the same and the Other through acts of discourse. To understand this text, and specifically to understand Watt's increasingly strange language, is in some ways to be forced to "appropriate," to borrow from Paul Ricoeur's essay "Appropriation," a discourse, to put it plainly, that may resist understanding as it resists reason as the discourse of "madness" (the Other): we are in a very real sense constrained to understand something that may construct itself *ex nihilo*. If one takes seriously the "meaning to be read" aspect of the aesthetic, however, a translation is inescapable, indeed obligatory: we are compelled by the exigencies of desire for understanding literally to translate Watt's discourse here (as I have done in the above quotation). We "speak" (appropriate) Watt as we translate, just as we speak Watt as we read the text in its entirety.

These moments of heightened translation are crucial, however, because we are here made fully conscious of this process of conferred appropriation. As we trace the complexities of Watt's discourse we begin to feel the full impact of the strangeness of his thought processes: it is here that Beckett succeeds most masterfully at violating and closing rapidly the discrete distance the reader has from this text: Watt as Other, or the Other's discourse, no longer functions *as* the alien, the Stranger (again to use Levinas). And of course, a final effect of this process of translation is our heightened awareness of Watt's own failure to translate Knott's discourse: the reader is compelled to effect what Watt is entirely unable or unwilling to do. After each example of Watt's reordering, Sam makes a comment similar to this: "Thus I missed I presume much I suppose of great interest touching I presume the third stage of the second or closing period of Watt's stay in Mr. Knott's house" (164). Watt's narrator—his witness—is denied full access to the story of Mr. Knott. After each new reordering, Sam asserts that he soon grows used to Watt's manner of speech. Ultimately, however, after the final expression of Watt's language—the description of the form of which takes approximately half a page (166–67)—Sam says: "I recall no example of this manner" (167). Although Sam immediately asserts that he again grew "used" to Watt's language, he admits that his hearing "now began to fail" (167) and in fact that he understood "one half of what won its way past my tympa" (167). Sam is, like Watt himself, an "imperfect witness" who cannot relate examples of Watt's final—and presumably most crucial—utterances. Watt fails to witness to Sam, who in turn fails to witness to us. Language has meaning only as it is understood; in Levinasian terms, the face of the Other is recognized and acknowledged only as it is *seen*.[8] My reading of Watt's use of language is intended to suggest that he is attempting not in the Beckettian mode to *express* what cannot be expressed but an effort, perhaps spurred on by the trauma of confronting the unwitnessable, the unnamable, to *become* what he cannot understand. And if the reader is obliged to read Watt's translation of

Knott, Watt bypasses that responsibility by collapsing the distance between self and Other. It is my sense, however, that this collapse of (rhetorical/linguistic) distance is ultimately, and in the full sense of the term, *meaningless,* because a full ethical recognition of the Other (Knott) cannot be realized by Watt.

My metahermeneutic reading of *Watt* is a conflation of two sources: Watt's interpretive development and the critical reception of *Watt*. My reading is orthodox hermeneutics in the sense that I have taken seriously Gadamer's notion that readings are "historical" insofar as they are made up of and react to previous readings. Watt's development as reader takes direction initially from a reading of substitution of form for content to a gradual acquiescence to semiotic free play. At the opposite pole is the general critical recourse to allegory, which, as I have suggested, expresses formally the desire to halt the insidious free play of *Watt;* allegory expresses the force of a desire for exorcism by explanation. These two poles of reading, I suggest, shift between reading of part (Watt's reading of Knott) and whole (allegory reducing the text wholly to one frame) without ever meeting successfully. My notion of allegory of reading and phronesis effects, I think, a successful dialectical negotiation between part and whole: it plays the dialectic between discrete event and whole in a way that at once acknowledges process (whole) and moment (discrete scenes of reading). Allegory of reading and hermeneutics are interpretive lenses that can make "sense" of individual acts of reading within the larger context of the narrative in a way that "simple" allegory (Watt as Christ, for example) cannot do: simple allegory can never fully explain discrete acts of reading as intrinsic elements of the larger allegorical movement of narrative. Allegory, in short, can never fully maintain the crucial balance between surface and depth that Beckett's texts continually demand: we can never lose sight of the "facticity" of the Beckett text in the haze of allegory, for to do so is, I suggest, ultimately to lose sight of the reader.[9]

Watt's hermeneutic interaction with Knott and Knott's world raises the interpretive questions that will of necessity haunt the reader of the Beckett oeuvre: it is a question of the limits and boundaries of interpretation. The relationship between Watt and Knott "translates" (as metaphor) into the reader's own interaction with the Beckett text. I do not wish to read *Watt* entirely as a hermeneutic cautionary tale, but Watt's reading and ultimate refusal of reading should alert the reader of Beckett to the specific problematics of interpretation as they arise in the dialogue or hermeneutical conversation with the Beckett text. Do we read the text allegorically: do we assert that this text really "is" about this or that? Or do we assert that nothing can be asserted and place the text simply in endless free play? The alternative is the one I have suggested above, that is, that we see in the text an allegory of reading itself. This reading is not mere allegory, however: as a hermeneutic process, it acknowledges simultaneously the internal coherence of the thematics of reading as it acknowledges our own continually shifting reading of that reading. I have attempted to demonstrate through my analysis of three "scenes" of reading that Watt's hermeneutic *develops* over the course of the text: within these readings we hear echoes and see shimmers of all major modes of reading that have been applied to *this* specific text, Beckett's *Watt*. Part of my understanding—my metahermeneutic understanding—of this text is that it posits itself, as a kind of *allegory* of reading, both as mirror and parody of the modes and means of its own decipherment: Beckett's well-known habit of inscribing the text's reading within its own discursive space is, I think, writ parodically large in *Watt,* and thus any one mode of reading, from allegory to a positing of semiotic free play, is already inscribed and to a degree neutered or threatened with redundancy. The result is, I think, a text that compels the reader away from asserting a specific hermeneutic even as it makes the reader complicit in the hermeneutic act. And it is finally the reader's task to acknowledge the "logic" of a contradictory, aporetic hermeneutic. Indeed, the text, by inscribing its own reading, collapses the hermeneutic distinction between Watt and reader, who, like Watt, must sift through mediating layers of polysemy and who is "thrown" by Watt's estranging discourse into an awareness of this conscious process of reading. But it is, finally, this awareness of reading that begins to demarcate the ontological gap between Watt and reader, the reader who, by effecting readings impossible for Watt, acts as a kind of specular hermeneutic "supplement" that works in the excesses of the semiotic void to articulate that void.

2

Mercier and Camier

> By what token shall we know the truth?
> —*Mercier and Camier*

Mercier and Camier represents Beckett's continual experimentation with what I call the discourse of specularity; where in *Watt*, the hermeneutic and specular quest of Watt to a degree articulates the reader into the text, in *Mercier and Camier* it is not the main characters who present themselves as mirrors of the reader's hermeneutic desire. It is onto the narrative—and, more precisely, the narrator—that the reader's specular hermeneutic desire is projected and, most important, diffused. To explore this diffusion of hermeneutic and narrative desire I will trace the role of the narrative voice in *Mercier and Camier* and how it articulates itself in the space between narrative and metanarrative. *Mercier and Camier* frames itself narratologically as an expression of hermeneutic desire; this desire is projected onto a diegetic plane that is split, constructing itself in a balance between narrative and metanarrative, into two discrete semiotic "zones." I will use Emile Benveniste's model of narrative, outlined in his essay "The Correlations of Tense in the French Verb," specifically his opposition between *histoire* (narrative) and *discours* (metanarrative), as a means to locate the affect of this text. In *histoire,* writes Benveniste, "events seem to narrate themselves" (208): the transparent narrative occults any sign of a narrator. In *discours* the narrator "proclaims himself as the speaker" (209) and thus removes the illusion of transparency in the metanarrative act.

I am interested here in part to gauge the effect of these differing "planes of utterance" (Benveniste 209) as they function within the single diegetic space of *Mercier and Camier.* I am reading Benveniste's distinction between *histoire* and *discours* as analogous to the distinction between narrative and metanarrative: the tension in *Mercier and Camier* is created by competing narrative modes attempting to inhabit the same discursive space. Benveniste's opposition also makes some sense of the manner in which Beckett uses intertextuality in this novel. Benveniste's distinction between *histoire* and *discours* is an attempt to locate subjectivity within modes of speech. In *histoire*, he suggests, we are in the historical utterance, the "narrative of past events" (206); here there is no sense of a speaker, no interference of the subject: "No one speaks here" (208). *Discours,* on the other hand, "assum[es] a speaker and a hearer" (209) and is the antithesis of objective historical documentation. I find a crucial resonance in the fact that Beckett's text combines modes of *histoire* and *discours* to problematize Benveniste's opposition. I also find a crucial resonance in the way Beckett's text locates the "historical" past within the intertext, within that mode, I argue, that functions analogously to the function of *discours* (the mode Benveniste argues cannot transcribe the historical). As I explain in detail below, Beckett's intertextuality effects a kind of "moving out" of the text, heightening the reader's awareness of the textuality of the text. Beckett's historical understanding—and intertextuality is for me a relation to history—works like the metanarrative moment, increasing our awareness of texts and responsibility to text.

Taken together these modes of narrative (*histoire/discours;* narrative/ metanarrative; text/intertextuality) express a doubly encoded desire for what I call "order," or what Ricoeur in "Appropriation" calls "directedness"; yet both serve to undermine the respective authority of the opposing discourse: this modal (self-)contradiction makes up the rhetorical effect of the novel. Through an examination of three instances of the metatextual figure in the novel, I suggest that the narrator decomposes, if not deconstructs, the narrative opposition between *histoire* and *discours* even as he attempts to maintain the autonomy of both semiotic zones. *Mercier and Camier* in turn enfolds the reader in a doubly encoded desire, the main textual expression of which is found not so much in a single character's expression as in the metanarrative coding within chapters, and between chapters, and in the summaries. It is the dialectical relationship between narrative and metanarrative that is the crux of the hermeneutical matter here.

This split between *histoire* and *discours* is perhaps the result of the text's particular narrative structure. *Mercier and Camier* (though not published until 1970) is the last text that maintains a split between the narrative (*Mercier and Camier*) and the narrated (Mercier and Camier). After *Mercier and Camier* we move into the increasing closeness or proximity of narrative and narrated as Beckett begins to employ the first person narrative voice: the result of this experimentation is what Beckett himself calls the "narrator/narrated." The sense of narrative anxiety in the trilogy—the desire, in part, to order events—(evident in *Mercier and Camier* in the chapter summaries and what I call metanarrative or metatextual "figures" or "gloss") is elided into the narrator/narrative itself and thus narrative anxiety (or desire) and hermeneutic anxiety (or desire) meet and join.

Mercier and Camier is most often read generically as it places itself within and against the canon of all previous "journey" or "quest" texts. Critics frequently comment on the generic position(ing) of *Mercier and Camier* because reading the novel, for instance, as a "journey-text" allows the critic to assert "order through intertext." Again, I read the critical reception of *Mercier and Camier* in part as a kind of anxiety formation. In this brief summary of critical (re)ordering of *Mercier and Camier* I will outline the way critics tend to be blind to the way the ruthlessly parodic nature of the text subverts at every step any hermeneutic intertextual control or ordering. Beckett's placing his text within the genre of the journey-text while subverting the genre sets up a disjunction that continually uses the reader's expectations against him or her; but, as continually, the specter of previous genres shimmers beneath this text, offering and encouraging the reader's desire for a "readerly" text. Again, although it is common to suggest that Beckett rewrites the genre, rarely are the full diegetic or semiotic implications of this fact *theorized*.

James Liddy in "Island Truancies: The Sauntering of Mercier and Camier" sees Mercier and Camier as "primal types" (44) whose "constant energy is transformed into a protest against all regulation" (44); the text is a parodic "anti-epic" concerned with tracing the saunterings of what Liddy calls "newly created souls": "*Mercier and Camier* bears a strange and untypical fruitfulness in the oeuvre of Beckett, in which is adumbrated the idea of an almost religious progress in the individual soul, and the patina of obsolescence that bestows elegance on random adventures" (48). The critic's recourse to allegory again appears as does the tendency to read the journey of Mercier and Camier in the (ordering) context of previous (textual) journeys. Thus Eric P. Levy, who, in *Beckett and the Voice of Species*, categorizes *Mercier and Camier* as a "pivotal exercise" (39), reads the text through the *Divine Comedy* seeing *Mercier and Camier* superimposed on the earlier work. The teleological purposefulness of Dante's work highlights the essentially aleatory world of Mercier and Camier. John Fletcher in *The Novels of Samuel Beckett* writes that *Mercier and Camier* ("a kind of hiatus between [the nouvelles] and *Molloy*" [118]) is "chiefly interesting as the first thorough working out of the journey theme that crops up next in *Molloy*" (118).

What is important about these critical readings of *Mercier and Camier* is the almost universal acknowledgment of the need for a particular "deflective" hermeneutic gesture. To read this text properly, these critics implicitly argue, is to read it through the genres it artfully rewrites or subverts. Ruby Cohn in *Back to Beckett* too sees the vital link between *Mercier and Camier* and the genre of the journey text: "In the novel itself, incidents are narrated only to dissolve without sequence; the caused effects of traditional fiction disappear, though the skeletal quest remains" (63). J. E. Dearlove in *Accommodating the Chaos* writes: "Although his works may never proffer completed conventional structures his pieces depend on the reader's perceptions of the disparity between the recognizable fragments he is given and the traditions they deliberately do not fulfill. The 'failures' of Mercier and Camier's trip or of Moran's report are evident only in contrast to our unsatisfied expectations about the nature of the quest or detective report" (41). In *The Solipsistic Novels of Samuel Beckett* Susan Schurman draws particular attention away from the form of the text's manipulation of the journey topos to the peculiar nature of the narrative voice; she still maintains, however, that the novel's efficacy is precipitated by and through the reader's expectations of narrative convention: "The reader's expectations are supposed to be disappointed. He is being shown the uselessness and extinction of an all-knowing, ubiquitous narrator in a world where knowledge is unattainable" (13).

I perhaps do not need to point out the degree to which intertextual (or intergeneric) readings of *Mercier and Camier,* like the overtly allegorical readings of *Watt* (which share a genetic link to intertextual hermeneutics), are the expression of another kind of interpretive anxiety. It seems that the critic cannot leave Mercier and Camier in the throes of a "failed" journey; to do so is to leave the reader in that uncomfortable state of anxiety that arises when confronted with disjunctive form.

My difficulty with a great deal of what has been written about *Mercier and Camier* is twofold. This deflective reading gesture seems problematical to me inasmuch as it threatens to reduce this text merely to the sum of its intertextual parts; thus when Dearlove writes that our awareness of narrative "failure" (whatever that means) arises "*only* in contrast to our unsatisfied expectations about the nature of the quest" (emphasis added), what I have called the "facticity" of the text is wholly ignored; the gloss (that is, the text's metanarrative), which, according to my reading, indicates a desire for order and thus presents itself as an implicit or tacit sign of narrative "failure" (desire being desire because never fulfilled) provides the means of perceiving a kind of narrative unease or potential "failure." In the critics' readings, thus, we have an explicit instance of a favoring of critical ordering over critical reading.

Any sustained theorizing of Beckettian intertextuality is absent in these, it seems to me, purely formal descriptions of Beckett's "parasitical" textual praxis. As I suggest, it is important to notice the inexorable "tension" between text and intertext in Beckett, the sense that parody requires the original text's "presence" in the intertext. If any subversion of the originating text (Dante, for instance) occurs, the nature of the parody dialectically requires that originating "horizon" as, paradoxically, a stabilizing force to be destabilized. Ultimately, my suggestion is that Beckett's intertextual praxis (perhaps like all intertextuality) never fully overturns the originating text even as the process of textual "subversion" occurs (this, of course, being Bakhtin's suggestion in *Rabelais*). I absolutely agree that this text articulates itself in the space of the intertext. But this tension between order and the aleatory—found in the relationship between text and intertext—imbricates itself into the primary level of diegesis. It is crucial to gauge the way in which the rhetorical effect of intertextuality is anticipated (and perhaps annulled) in the text's manipulation of the play of *histoire* and *discours*. I suggest that the ultimate rhetorical effect of Beckett's intertextuality (like the effect of metanarrative generally) is a "moving out" from *histoire* proper, a momentary alienation from the text itself. Critics are correct to suggest that Beckett's intertextuality is "ironic," that it points up the distance between historically specific modes of reference, meaning, and understanding. My take on this irony is different, however. To spend time gauging the effect of this distance, to see how Beckett's text does not fulfill the traditions it refers to, is I think to fall into a rhetorical trap. It is a given, an a priori, that the Beckett text cannot fulfill the traditions of the past, that it is in some ways "posthuman" and thus beyond easy categories of humanism. To theorize the precise relation between, for example, Christopher Marlowe's *Faustus* and Mercier's quotation from that text (I examine this moment below) is to suggest a relation that by definition cannot be sustained. We are correct to notice how the intertext moves us away from *Mercier and Camier* proper; but the precise nature of this "ex-centricity" needs to be theorized. I thus emphasize the need for an initial formulation or account of this text's own diegetic/semiotic splitting before deflecting our hermeneutic interests to individual sites of intertextual interest.

I have isolated in my reading of *Mercier and Camier* three types of narrative *discours* (that is, figures of narrative self-exposure). The first type overtly calls attention to the artifice of the narrative through ostensive markers. The second is more difficult to place under a clear rubric of *discours* as it seems to imbricate itself as closely as possible over the mode of *histoire;* that is, in particular instances in the text, both modes of narrative seem to inhabit the same discursive space. The third type is that found in the summaries themselves and in the two lists found in the narrative proper (pages 23–72). I will proceed to look closely at all three instances of the metatextual figure in *Mercier and Camier* to suggest the complexity of Beckett's manipulation of this textual rhetoric. Each "type" of metatextual figure is similar in that all act as a kind of "gloss" on the narrative proceedings proper (*histoire*), commenting on, ordering, or asserting the essential instability of the entire process. Each figure too is important as it plays out within itself the crucial and, for Beckett it seems, fundamentally problematic opposition between *histoire* and *discours*. I am interested in exploring these figures of narrative self-exposure in *Mercier and Camier* precisely to examine the rhetorical effect of the narrator's reaction to his own narrative on our reading of it. I wish always to keep foregrounded the manner in which these moments are communicated, that is, the narratological filter through which we are presented with the text's reading of itself.[1] In one sense I wish to suggest how these moments provide, tacitly or explicitly, and perhaps ironically, the means for the text's entire reading.

The first sentence of *Mercier and Camier* sets the unstable tone of the entire narrative: "The journey of Mercier and Camier is one I can tell, if I will, for I was with them all the time" (7). The sentence turns on this "if I will," a phrase that gives a sense of absolute conditionality ("if") continually offset by what I read as the will-to-narrative of this oftentimes intrusive narrator. His "for I was with them" is a patent red herring, a claim—if true, but does it really matter *if* it is true?—undermined at every turn by the narrator's steady stream of doubt as to the credibility of his own narrative. The maneuver in this opening statement is a rhetorical prelude to the entire narrative. The narrative voice here presents a willed (that is, constructed) narrative only to suggest its instability and its overt constructedness. The reader is at the mercy of this slightly peevish narrator for his or her definition of the journey: I think it vital to keep the "origins" of our knowledge of Mercier and Camier fully foregrounded here, for we build on shifting sands if we assert anything absolute about this story.

Indeed, it is with the function of knowledge and knowing (as well as telling) in the narrative voice that I am concerned in this chapter. While it is true, as most commentators suggest, that this "I" seems to disappear after this opening salvo, it is important to follow his progress as he "traces" the journey of Mercier and Camier, for it is he who, if anyone, negotiates the reader's proximity to the text: it is he ultimately who will begin to articulate the reader's response to the story. It is his narrative, which enfolds the reader in this doubly encoded desire for narrative and knowledge. And, contrary to critical opinion, moreover, the narrator does never fully disappear like some half-witted *deus absconditus*. He is everywhere "read" through his metatextual comments on Mercier and Camier's actions. It is he who tells us that Mercier and Camier were "driven by a need now clear and now obscure" (7); yet it is also he who, after describing the "meeting" of Mercier and Camier, writes, "What stink of artifice" (9). This phrase is the first overt metatextual sign in the text and requires, I think, some consideration because it has some fairly complex resonances. The phrase follows the summary of Mercier and Camier's chance missings:

	Arr.	Dep.	Arr.	Dep.	Arr.	Dep.	Arr.
Mercier	9.05	9.10	9.25	9.30	9.40	9.45	9.50
Camier	9.15	9.20	9.35	9.40	9.50	(9)	

The comment seems to refer deictically to this grid (a grid semiotically analogous to the chapter summaries) and thus suggests at first that any textual ordering of occurrences is an imposition of an artificial plot. But because the grid functions as a kind of summary—or narrative—of Mercier and Camier's saunterings to this point it also bears an analogous ontological resemblance to the entirety of the narrative the narrator chooses to tell. Thus the comment, which resounds into the entire novel as it removes the illusion of a self-generating narrative, has a deep philosophical import and suggests an essential, and perhaps unbridgeable, ontological gap between action and account, between event and narrative.

This philosophical position is, however, problematized as we encounter other remarks of the narrator such as "Certain things shall never be known for sure" (10) or "In any case nothing is known for sure, henceforth" (103). The reader is caught in a double bind between what appears to be an ordering narrative/narrator—one who tacitly suggests his own hand in the creation of the journey ("artifice")—and one who admits ignorance of purpose, meaning, and telos. The complication here is more involved, I think, than Schurman suggests in her emphasis on the extinction of an all-knowing narrator. The difficulty is that the narrator is at once able to order, structure, and form the story (however aleatory it may appear) and to maintain an ignorance about certain things.[2] The complication is that the narrator is not extinct *enough*. The reader's position in *Mercier and Camier* thus may be formulated into a question: how do we read a narrative at once tacitly self-confident ("What stink of artifice") and overtly unsure of itself? The question is further and perhaps more precisely, *What* do we read in this aporetic narrative? I return to Camier's anticipatory question: "By what token shall we know the truth?"

The narrator of *Mercier and Camier* often returns to this particular destabilizing metatextual figuring. In chapter 7, for example, he foregrounds the text's foundational instability by offering the reader a hand in deciding certain elements of plot: "A road still carriageable climbs over the high moorland. It cuts across vast turfbogs, a thousand feet above sealevel, two thousand if you prefer" (97); the passage ends with this blithe comment: "It is here one would lie down, in a hollow bedded with dry heather, and fall asleep, for the last time, on an afternoon, in the sun, head down among the minute life of stems and bells, and fall fast asleep, fast farewell to charming things. It's a birdless sky, the odd raptor, no song. End of descriptive passage" (98). The entire passage is bracketed by these two statements, the first of which explicitly offers the reader a "choice" in the description, the second of which acts as a jolt to the readerly sensibility that may have become lulled by the narrator's evocative prose.

Much has been made of this text's self-undermining rhetoric, and the first statement here gives the illusion of instability some credibility by imparting a sense of a potentially protean text: it does not really matter, this statement suggests, if the moorland is one thousand or two thousand feet. What matters for the reader and for narratological purposes, however, is that the moorland *could* be either one thousand or two thousand feet. The second statement—"End of descriptive passage"—acts as a kind of *Verfremdungseffekt*, shocking the reader into an awareness of the facticity of text and the facility with which the narrator can lull the reader into a sense of "another" world. These statements, then, would seem, like the previous "What stink of artifice," to undermine the "reality" or illusion of the narrative, to foreground explicitly the process of (con)fabulation. It is, I think, at this point that most critics end their analysis of the semiology of the metatextual figure or gloss. It is, however, crucial to keep in mind the dialectical (one might say parasitical) nature of these moments. *If* the figures undermine prior description *as* description they still require the presence of the "prior" text—the descriptive passage, for example—from and to which to orient their rhetorical effects.

There is thus a curiously interdependent quality of relationship between *discours* and *histoire* in these metatextual figures. The point I am making here originates in my reading of Beckett's manipulation of the rhetoric or discourse (in Benveniste's sense of *discours* pointing deictically to the present moment of narrative enunciation) of the metatext. The text proceeds—on a metatextual level—only in fits and starts; the metanarrative voice enters at moments only seemingly to refine itself out of existence at the next. A perfect emblem of this effect—if it is not a technique—is the paragraph opening chapter 7 cited above. The impression left by this rhetoric of "reader's choice" and self-aware manipulation of the *Verfremdungseffekt* is not a total effacing of the rhetoric of (literary) realism. It seems as if each side of the equation here a<—>b (a: self-conscious narrator; b: realistic detail) is given equal weight and the reader is left with each "discourse" shimmering in a perpetual balance of what Gadamer in *Truth and Method* calls "open indeterminacy" (340).

I suggest also that it is here, in the recognition of the interdependent relation between *histoire* and *discours*, that an analogy with Beckett's manipulation of intertextuality should be made. There is a curious dependence between *histoire* and *discours*: one needs the other to orient its rhetorical effects and ultimately the relationship produces a vertiginous kind of uncertainty. *Discours*—the rhetoric of the metanarrative—produces a centripetal effect, a moving outward from the illusion of pure narrative. In Linda Hutcheon's terms, the effects of *discours* are "ex-centric" (*A Poetics of Postmodernism)*: there is a moving out of the centered text, a moving away from stability. Beckett's intertextuality, perhaps like all forms of intertextuality, is also a moving away. When, for instance, we read in the second chapter that "All their judgements relating to the expedition called for revision, in tranquillity" (24) and register the allusion to Wordsworth, we are no longer strictly speaking "in" Beckett's text: like the moment of *discours,* the allusion is alienating, shocks us into an awareness of other texts, of a *history* of textuality that feeds into Beckett's text. And with the recognition of the allusion comes the responsibility for doing something with the quotation: for recognizing, for instance, the irony of the implicit comparison between Mercier and Camier and Wordsworth's poet. Or, perhaps less ironically but no less complicating, we are to recognize the aptness of the implicit comparison between two common men and the poet who is to speak the language of the common man. At any rate, these moments of intertextuality effect a pause, inscribe a moment of the historical, an intertextual spot in time.

Examples of Beckett's intertextuality abound in *Mercier and Camier,* some more complicated than others. I suggested in my introduction to this chapter that the common critical reading of Beckett's intertextuality is to see a parodic subversion of an originating text (Dante being a common intertext). I believe that we need to recognize that Beckett's intertext is more nuanced than some suggest: each intertext seems to me to be carefully weighed in the balance before being committed to the page; each intertext can be read in contradictory ways; each intertext is highly polysemous and as such can never be fully categorized. What, for instance, are we to make of one of the text's more obscure allusions, in this case to Marlowe's *Faustus*?

> I was thinking of saying something, said Mercier, but on second thoughts I'll keep it to myself.
> Selfish pig, said Camier.
> Go on you, said Mercier.
> Where was I? said Camier.
> Let our watchword be, said Mercier.
> Ah yes, said Camier, lente, lente, and circumspection, with deviations to right and left and sudden reversals of course. (67)

The allusion here ("lente, lente") is to Marlowe's *Faustus*, specifically to Act V, scene ii, in which Faustus appeals for night to run slowly (he has one day to live). The full quotation is *"lente, lente, currite noctis equi"* and is a quotation from Ovid's *Amores:* the intertext is doubled, as it were. Are we thus to read Mercier and Camier as Faustian figures? As Ovidian lovers wishing the night never to end so they can remain together forever? As parodies of these figures? Like all of Beckett's pseudo-couples, there are elements of a lover's pact in the relationship between Mercier and Camier as well as perhaps a Faustian bargain: constant, yet inexorable, companionship. I have suggested that the play of *histoire* and *discours* produces an open indeterminacy, that it is impossible to see one rhetorical figure assuming a position of ultimate authority. The same can be said about the text-intertext relationship: the relationship—indeed, like the relationship of Beckett's pseudo-couples—is symbiotic: one is necessary to the other, one cannot exist without the other. Questions of authority, whether rhetorical or otherwise, seem strangely out of place here: to ascribe to the Beckett text the authority to "subvert" a preceding text is to ascribe a character—or text—full discursive power. How do we reconcile Beckett's professed "inability to express" with the power to subvert literary tradition?

Moreover, this question of intertextuality is attenuated by the equally problematic question of Beckett's practice of intratextuality, that is, his practice of referring to work within his own corpus. Intratextuality too is a movement outward but is a movement out to another location within the same body. Perhaps the most important intratext in *Mercier and Camier* is to *Watt*. Among the characters in *Mercier and Camier* are Mr. Graves, the gardener in *Watt*, and Mr. Gall, whose musings on the ontology of pianos and piano tuners form a crucial moment in *Watt*, as I argued in the previous chapter. Bringing characters from other of his texts is a common practice in Beckett's early to middle work (the trilogy has a heavy intratextual component). The effect is not unlike that of intertextuality. It suggests that to grasp the full effect of the Beckett texts requires a knowledge of the history of his *oeuvre*. The appearance of Watt at the end of *Mercier and Camier* is crucial in that he acts both as a reminder of past texts (Mercier says that Watt reminds him of Murphy) and as a prophet looking forward to the texts of the future; Watt describes himself as one on a quest: "I too have sought, said Watt, all on my own, only I thought I knew what. Can you beat that one? . . . One shall be born, said Watt, one is born of us, who having nothing will wish for nothing, except to be left the nothing he hath" (113–14). This is a complex historical moment for the reader familiar with the trilogy and the Unnamable, who seems to be the one described here. Allusions to the plays are also present in *Mercier and Camier* and produce a similar historical resonance. We can see a consistency of theme over the years (if we choose) by reading Watt's "Fuck life!" (118) against *Rockaby*'s final line. We can read *Mercier and Camier*—as many critics in fact do—as a pretext for *Waiting for Godot* and thus gauge the resonance of lines like "Nothing to be done" (87) or themes like the refusal of communicating dreams (61) against the play. I wonder about the effect of these intratextual allusions, however. One is tempted to see them as evidence of a consistency of theme over the years, a working out of a common field of ideas. I think this approach demands a holistic view of the entire corpus and tends to obscure the effects within the originary text, the text that is formed in this web of allusions. The effect is of a moving outward, narratively and, I would argue, subjectively. A crucial effect here is the sense that the subjectivity of the Beckett character is dependent—in a sense genetically—on his precursor; that is, that the character is an amalgam, a plurality of subjectivities. And the narrative itself thus comes to be seen as an amalgam of narratives, texts dependent on their precursors. There is thus a clear suggestion of the relation between narrative and subjectivity, as if Beckett is concretizing the notion that we are the sum of the narratives we inhabit or that inhabit us.

These inter/intra/textual moments—like the narrative play of *discours*—work at a crucial level of temporality, historical and narrative. The inter/intratext compels a recognition of the literary historical past, functions, I suggest, as a stepping out of the present narrative moment. In turn, the recognition of the literary historical past compels a recognition of the textuality of the present work: *Mercier and Camier* is a story aware of itself as a story (with a past). Inter/intratextual allusions do not, as far as I can tell, function to subvert the literary past but to suggest a leveling out of *priority*. Subversion suggests that something has the power to subvert or the authority to claim the need to be subverted. In Beckett no such authority can exist because no such priority can exist: the words of Ovid, Marlowe, Wordsworth, and Beckett in the mouths of Mercier and Camier are simply random words, words without authority.

The second type of metatextual figure occurs infrequently in *Mercier and Camier* but bears a vital relation to the thematics of the dialectic of *discours* and *histoire*. A couple of examples will serve to demonstrate the difficulty of reading these metatextual moments. At the beginning of chapter 2 Mercier and Camier are in the midst of a crowd "pressed on as towards some unquestioned goal" (21). They pause and the following exchange occurs:

> You hinder me more than you help me, said Mercier.
> I'm not trying to help you, said Camier, I'm trying to help myself.
> Then all is well, said Mercier.
> I'm cold, said Camier.
> It was indeed cold.
> It is indeed cold, said Mercier. (21)

I will excerpt the second example before returning to the above; in chapter 5, Mercier and Camier arrive at Helen's home:

> Night was falling. They prowled about the centre, at a loss where to go. Finally, at the suggestion of Mercier, whose turn it must have been to lead, they went to Helen's. She was in bed, a trifle unwell, but rose none the less and let them in, not without having first cried, from behind the door, Who goes there? They told her all the latest, their hopes both shattered and forlorn. They described how they had been chased by the bull. She left the room and came back with the umbrella. Camier manipulated it at length. But it's in perfect trim, he said, quite perfect. I mended it, said Helen. . . . It opens like a dream,

said Camier, and when I release—click!—the catch it collapses unaided. I open, I close, one, two, click, plop, click, pl—. Have done, said Mercier, before you break it on us again. I'm a trifle unwell, said Helen. (70)

In the first example, the initial "it was indeed cold" seems discursively to indicate the presence of the narrator unmediated by his role *as* narrator: it is as if, perhaps, seeing as he was "with them all the time" (7), the comment is the remark of the narrator at the time of the incident (story time). Mercier's repetition of the same comment, like Helen's "I'm a trifle unwell," down to the slightly pretentious qualifier "indeed" (Helen's "trifle" works in the same manner to mark her comment as a "quotation") acts, however, to suggest the absence of the narrator at that moment (unless we wish to characterize Mercier as a congenital idiot merely repeating what is said by others, the moment has more complex resonances). What we have here is an uncanny—this is the term for the effect here—meeting and (seeming) blend of *histoire* and *discours,* as if Mercier is privy to the machinations of the extranarrative ordering force (the narrator), or, conversely, the narrator again is simply and perversely exposing the processes of his creation. These moments act to stop the forward movement of the narrative, forcing the reader to look back on what he has read and think through the implications of "self"-quotation. The first lines, "It was indeed cold," "She was in bed, a trifle unwell" which initially and fairly comfortably occupy the space of *histoire,* are read retrospectively as quoted lines and thus as ostensive markers of the narrator's discursive presence. There is a blurring here as these lines seem—and perhaps these too are moments of undecidability—simultaneously to occupy both spaces of *histoire* and *discours,* indicating both the presence and absence of the narrator as *he* indicates the present moment of enunciation only to withdraw all markers of that presence. The effect here—and this is admittedly only a possible reading of a complex narrative device—is ultimately to suggest and place Mercier and Camier as playthings, puppets dangling discursively at the diegetic whim of the narrator.

I mentioned at the outset of this chapter that *Mercier and Camier* was split between two discrete semiotic "zones." I think the above analysis illustrates the reader's obligation to maintain both the discourse of realism and the rhetoric of the metanarrative (which I am positing as each occupying and articulating a distinct "zone" of hermeneutic obligation) in a kind of balance while proceeding through the text. Both discourses taken together represent for me the narratological crux of the matter here. I posited above that the text articulates itself on a dialectical axis of instability and a desire for order. In my reading this dialectic plays out in the uncomfortable paratactical arrangement of *histoire* and *discours*: the rhetoric of realism—as traditional mode of totalizing narrative—is continually "threatened" or exposed *as* rhetorical construct and as driven by desire (for order) by the rhetorical maneuvers of the self-conscious metanarrator, whose *discours* in turn is exposed *as discours* by the rhetoric of realism.

I have demonstrated this disjunction or clash of narrative mode in the space of the "main" narrative here in *Mercier and Camier*. It thus remains to explore the rhetorical or discursive effect of the third type of metatextual figure on our reading of this fractured text. The summaries are semiotically analogous to the two lists presented (perhaps by the narrator) in the "main" narrative of *Mercier and Camier*. Indeed, both serve similar purposes and both are as difficult to locate narratologically. I have thus far assumed that the summaries are presented ("spoken" seems to go too far) by the narrator himself. Is this, however, a valid claim? I think I can illustrate this problem by exploring briefly the semiotic of the two lists in *Mercier and Camier* using a question formulated by Barthes in *S/Z*. Barthes's question to Balzac's text is vital for our reading of Beckett's lists and summaries: "Who speaks?"[3] The first list appears in the second chapter and serves to summarize and focus the themes of the text:

1. It would be useless, nay, madness, to venture any further for the moment.
2. They need only ask Helen to put them up for the night.
3. Nothing would prevent them from setting out on the morrow, hail, rain or shine, at the crack of dawn.
4. They had nothing to reproach themselves with.
5. Did what they were looking for exist?
6. What were they looking for?
7. There was no hurry.
8. All their judgements relating to the expedition called for revision, in tranquillity.
9. Only one thing mattered: depart.
10. To hell with it anyway. (23–24)

This list, as list, acts to draw attention to itself as construct, as a kind of stepping out, or aside, of the narrative proper. It is another method of calling attention to the narrative's artifice, a way of asserting one thing only to withdraw it: "To hell with it all anyway." It also maintains the discursive presence of the narrator, who implies his "I" through the use of "they" and "their." The second list problematizes this seemingly clear relationship between narrator and "narratee." It appears in chapter 7 and is framed thus: "Finally a great light bathed their understandings, flooding in particular the following concepts":

1. The lack of money is an evil. But it can turn to a good.
2. What is lost is lost.
3. The bicycle is a great good. But it can turn nasty, if ill employed.
4. There is food for thought in being down and out.
5. There are two needs: the need you have and the need to have it.
6. Intuition leads to many a folly.
7. That which the soul spews forth is never lost.
8. Pockets daily emptier of their last resources are enough to break the stoutest resolution.
9. The male trouser has got stuck in a rut, particularly the fly which should be transferred to the crotch and designed to open trapwise, permitting the testes, regardless of the whole sordid business of micturition, to take the air unobserved. The drawers should of course be transfigured in consequence.
10. Contrary to a prevalent opinion, there are places in nature from which God would appear to be absent.
11. What would one do without women? Explore other channels.
12. Soul: another four-letter word.
13. What can be said of life not already said? Many things. That its arse is a rotten shot, for example. (72–73)

The list here is, from a grammatico-semiological perspective, qualitatively different from the previous one: there is (in the list proper) no grammatical indication of Mercier and Camier as "they" or "their" (I discount the general "you" in number 5); consequently, the narrator, as "I," seems to efface himself, as will happen in the summaries and does happen in the discourse of the epigram. The list, like Benveniste's *histoire*, seems to narrate itself. Yet both lists, like the chapter summaries, articulate a space for themselves within the narrative structure focusing the reader's attention on the narrative as "summarizable," as able to be halted for purposes of "reflection," that is, open to reevaluation and compression at any point

("All their judgements relating to the expedition called for revision, in tranquillity").

Like the lists, the summaries—which I have suggested act as a "gloss" on the main narrative—act initially to assert a spatio-temporal order or scheme over the meandering flow of Mercier and Camier's "journey": they, to use Ricoeur's phrase, attempt to assert "meaningful totalities out of scattered events" (278). As do all summaries, they act to consolidate and focus the narrative placement of the characters: they "clear" a space for the narrator to proceed even as he places the characters within space and time. The scheme is ordered "imagistically": the images themselves are arranged paratactically encouraging, perhaps, a (re)writerly response in the reader:

> VII
> The bog.
> The cross.
> The ruins.
> Mercier and Camier part.
> The return.
> VIII
> The life of afterlife.
> Camier alone.
> Mercier and Watt.
> Mercier, Camier and Watt.
> The last policeman.
> The last bar.
> Mercier and Camier.
> Lock Bridge.
> The arctic flowers.
> Mercier alone.
> Dark at its full. (123)

My reading of the summaries arises in part out of the idea that they stand to the original and originating text as a special type of "reading" or interpretation. We might even read the summaries using as a focus Roman Ingarden's notion of "concretization": the summaries bring into "being" a clear scheme out of what at times appears as random schemae.[4] The summaries do act to order, to focus, and to consolidate the temporal-spatial thrust of the narrative, but even as they articulate themselves, they highlight specific aspects of the narrative. The result for the reader is a text that "tells" itself twice, or, more precisely, attempts to tell itself twice: iteration always articulates itself in the space of difference. The difficulty for the reader, of course, is that, unlike instances of "reading" in *Watt* for instance, the summaries in this text do not overtly present themselves as "readings" to the reader. They act as a laying out of material to be read but fail to carry out that reading: the only "reading" in *Mercier and Camier* is the metatextual figures of the first type that I discussed. If the metatextual destabilizing of the narrative proper occurs, it is seemingly absent in the summaries: it is almost as if *this* discursive space bears all the responsibility for stabilizing the narrative.

Yet, of course, the summaries as gloss act metatextually in the same mode as the previously discussed figures "What stink of artifice" or "End of descriptive passage." It is this realization that exposes the summaries as containing the central contradiction of this text. The metatextual gloss as gloss asserts order or directedness as it clarifies; yet as gloss, that is, as iteration, the summaries expose the artifice of the text they rewrite. The text, being summarizable, thus has no real independent "priority" ("The whole question of priority, so luminous hitherto, is from now on obscure" [103]). Moreover, the summaries resolutely expose the *desire* for order as they mark themselves ostensively as summaries: they articulate themselves from within the space of "discursive" anxiety, tacitly acknowledging that order, or directedness, if it does not appear in the narrative proper, will appear in the semiotic zone of the summary. The summaries thus contain both (self-contradictory) drives that we explored in the narrative proper: the desire for order and the drive to expose that desire as desire and thus as artifice to be revealed, as it indeed is, *as* artifice. The summaries in fact seem to contain the maximum compression of the central aporia of *Mercier and Camier*.

And indeed we can return to the notion of Beckettian intratextuality here to further the complications of the summaries. The summaries, as shorthand references and repetitions of the original text (but this question of originality is, as I say, problematized), operate as quotations of the original, as mirrorings of the original. As radically compressed versions of the previous narrative, the summaries can also be read as parody, as exposing narrative simply as a series of occurrences, of images, without any real human interest: the human contact explored in the novel (or the failure of that contact) is reduced to a series of blank statements. But perhaps "parody" here is too strong a word. Parody, as Fredric Jameson reminds us in "Postmodernism and Consumer Society," requires a sense in the parodist of an "originality" in the text to be parodied, a sense of individual style, a continuous whole (194). Jameson also makes the important point that parody has as an ultimate effect a feeling of humor. While I maintain that *Mercier and Camier* is one of the most amusing of Beckett's works, that humor is not found in the summaries, which, in my view, read as rather pitiless—perhaps "disinterested" is a better word—statements of narrative plot. I see these moments rather in Jameson's terms as moments of *pastiche:* "Pastiche is, like parody, the imitation of a peculiar or unique style, the wearing of a stylistic mask, speech in a dead language: but it is a neutral practice of such mimicry, without parody's ulterior motive, without the satirical impulse, without laughter, without that still latent feeling that there exists something *normal* compared to which what is being imitated is rather comic" (195). Pastiche, Jameson goes on to say, is "blank parody" (195). I want to modify this idea and suggest that Beckett's summaries should be read as "blank interpretations," interpretations without obvious ulterior motive, interpretations that inscribe within themselves the grounds of their own dismantling. As in Beckett's practice of intertextuality—which serves not to parody the original but to set up an aporia of affect—the summaries, as intratext, produce an undecidability. Are they there to stabilize a random, chaotic text? Do they function to point out the ultimate purposelessness of Mercier and Camier's journey? Do they function to produce both effects in what Gadamer calls an "open indeterminacy"?

In some fashion the summaries do all these things. As specular reflections of the original text they refract as they reflect a complicated series of desires. I argue that specularity in Beckett has two interrelated components, both hinging on their relationship to desire: the first is when the text reflects (and refracts) the position of the actual reader, who is drawn into the text by means of a complex moment of recognition, recognizing an analogous relation to a character's puzzlement, anxiety, desire. The implications of this kind of mirroring become crucial when the character reflecting (and projecting) our desires is gradually dismantled, whether mentally or physically (an elaborate version of this kind of lethal specularity is played out in *Molloy*). Beckett explores a related type of mirroring in *Mercier and Camier:* here I would argue that the text functions to mirror itself to itself in such a way as to complicate the reader's response to it. These mirroring, echo effects—inter/intratextuality; the summaries—suggest a plurality of discourses threading through the Beckett text, a plurality ultimately productive of a number of competing, perhaps contradictory, desires. If in the Lacanian model of specularity the mirror functions as metaphor for identity formation, how are we to read a text that mirrors both the history of its precursors and its own structure as narrative? In other words, how do we read the impulse toward narcissism (intratextuality) and an outward reflection (intertextuality) inhabiting the same discursive space? One response would be that the Beckett text constructs its identity via a history that is ultimately neutered: intertextuality functioning neither to parody an original nor to stabilize a present text. Further, the narcissistic impulse suggests not a singularity of narrative—not one narrative continually being told—but a variety of repeated narratives within a whole. Both specular impulses produce a radical undecidability: (narrative) identity is not, for Beckett, to be found in the mirror of the past or in the self-reflective mirror. It is to be found in the contradiction formed as both impulses to the past and the narcissistic present are played out in the same narrative space.

The peculiar aporetic of the metatextual figure in *Mercier and Camier* will not be seen in the trilogy, where *histoire* and *discours* give way fully to *discours* as any illusion of the third person is effaced. *Mercier and Camier*, as I have here demonstrated, turns on the crux of the absence/presence dialectic of the narrator, and the reader thus is left to speculate on any number of issues, all of which, I think, can be distilled into one question: What is the effect of a self-summarizable text on the reader? a text not merely summarized, but—and this is a crucial refinement—*able* to be summarized within its own narrative space?

I think we can begin to pry open this question if we focus on the relationship between narrative and hermeneutics and the aporia of the narrator who attempts to but finally cannot "order" his text. My purpose here is merely to suggest—as a kind of preamble; this idea becomes fully formed in the trilogy—an essential link between narrative and hermeneutics, a link that articulates itself in the discursive structures of *Mercier and Camier*. I wish to "turn" the word "narrative" back to its etymological roots to suggest a link between narrative as an expression of a desire for knowledge, hence having an essential epistemological function, and as a desire to communicate (tell), hence having an essential narratological or diegetic function. "Narrative," as Hayden White reminds us in *The Content of the Form,* comes from gnarus and narro, both roots from the Sanskrit "gna," meaning knowing and telling. It is only after establishing the means or grounds of knowledge that a reading of that ordering can be made: thus—and I think this is precisely the narrator's discovery in

Mercier and Camier—the epistemological gesture (in this case, the ordering of the narrative) is sequentially, perhaps genetically, related to the hermeneutic gesture. I am here suggesting a link between epistemology and hermeneutics positing epistemology as the initial act of a totalizing hermeneutic gesture. The difficulty for the narrator of *Mercier and Camier* is that he cannot trust his own epistemologies: they are constructed only to be dismantled: "No knowing. No knowing such things anymore" (103). The narrator cannot bring himself to accept the "necessary illusion" of narrative as "knowing" and thus will not be able to offer any reading of "meaning" within that illusion.

# 3

Molloy

> For what happened was quite different.
> —*Molloy*

The trilogy represents the culmination of a number of narrative and hermeneutic threads in the early to middle phase of Beckett's oeuvre. It is here that the discourse of specularity is fully articulated as the reader's obligations to the text become fully formed. In my tracing of the metahermeneutic in *Watt* and the hermeneutic of narrative in *Mercier and Camier* I pointed out that the reader is always to a degree kept at a distance. In *Watt*, Beckett had not completely formed the structure of the specular reader and thus the reader's "role" as hermeneut was anticipated and "blocked" at specific moments of active hermeneutical inquiry: Beckett's manipulation of this specularity enabled the reader to maintain a relatively comfortable distance from any potential violation. *Mercier and Camier* finds the desire of reader—and desire is always the motivating force of the specular reader—diffused and scattered into a variety of discrete yet interpenetrating semiotic "zones." The aporia for the reader of *Mercier and Camier* is precisely that a dominant "role" or "zone" of reading is not defined, a result, as H. Porter Abbott suggests, of the mediation of a third person narrator.

In the trilogy the already perhaps tenuous opposition between *histoire* and *discours*—between first and third person narratives, between narrative and metanarrative—is eradicated as the first persons of Molloy, Malone, and the Unnamable assume diegetic control. Thus we can begin to frame the trilogy—and indeed a great deal of the post-trilogy prose and drama—as being microscopically concerned with the hermeneutics of the individual subject: these texts have as a central concern the interaction between the individual and, at least for Molloy—to a lesser and lessening extent, for Malone and the Unnamable—his immediate psychological and physical environment. The trilogy proceeds with the subject in increasing disintegrative crisis; the subject articulates himself along what David

Watson in *Paradox and Desire in Samuel Beckett's Fiction* calls a "sliding scale of narrative dispossession" (15). As he diminishes, a concomitant desire for narrative (as) hermeneutics takes over. This process begins with narratives of external events (Molloy) and gradually proceeds to one of claustrophobic self-interpretation (Malone, the Unnamable). The reader thus is confronted by three narratives of extreme self-consciousness and, as in reading *Mercier and Camier,* must continually balance between narrative and metanarrative, continually negotiating a hermeneutic space within which to read a consistently self-undermining narrative.

As the disintegration of the speaking subject occurs over the narratives of the trilogy, the reader's role and obligation is incrementally heightened: indeed, I might posit that one of the major "themes" of the trilogy *is* the increased awareness of text as read object. I must make it clear at the outset that I read these texts as a series because a thematics of reading is developed over the course of the three novels. In *Molloy* and *Malone Dies* the reader is confronted with the subject in crisis but still perhaps intact (if we read Molloy and Moran as discrete individuals rather than as two aspects of the same character, as has been suggested). Molloy and Malone attempt, moreover, to locate themselves in space and time; they can give specifics of geography, can trace their own progression through the narrative. In *The Unnamable,* however, the subject is in radical crisis, unable to fix himself *as* subject; he is unable, indeed, to narrate a coherent story: any clarifying semiotic or narrative signposts give way in the Unnamable's narrative. Consequently, the reader is left or presented with a greater degree of writerly responsibility. It is with mapping the incremental responsibility of the specular hermeneutic reader in the trilogy that the next chapters are concerned.

It is in the criticism of the trilogy that the thematics of reading as writing (as narrative) are fully explored and exploited; it is here that scrutiny is given to the intense textuality, or rhetoricity, of the text; and it is here, finally, that we see the (re)birth of the Beckettian reader. I have suggested that hermeneutics—which for me encompasses, or engulfs, textuality and narrative practice—was always a major focus in the early phase of Beckett's oeuvre. The trilogy, however, has an explicit and self-conscious academic tone (what Paul Davies in *The Ideal Real* calls "academic fussiness" [68]) that immediately signals and prompts "serious," perhaps philosophical, attention. Indeed, the Beckett critical community has framed the trilogy as the highest achievement in Beckett's prose fiction, not the least reason being because of its intense self-scrutiny as text and as read object.

Critics seem to focus primarily on two interpenetrating issues arising within the trilogy and in *Molloy* especially: both can be understood as dealing in some way with the thematics of the subject. The thematics of the subject will encompass the issue of narrative-making and the relationship between the two "parts" of *Molloy*, which really is an exploration of the "ontological" link between Molloy and Moran, that is, a continuation of the exploration of subjectivity in narrative. Hugh Kenner notes the link between the idea of the subject and the formation of narrative; in *A Reader's Guide to Samuel Beckett* he comments on Beckett's reformulation of the narrator-narrative binary into what Beckett has called the "narrator/narrated":

> It is a device he employs in all his subsequent fiction, bringing the ambient world into existence only so far as the man holding the pencil can remember it or understand it, so that no omniscient craftsman is holding anything back, and simultaneously bringing into existence the man with the pencil, who is struggling to create himself, so to speak, by recalling his own past or delineating his own present. (94)

The thematics of self-creation as narrative creation are picked up and echoed often in the corpus of the criticism. In *Accommodating the Chaos* Judith Dearlove writes: "Beneath the apparent and artificial diversity of traditional associations is the universal figure of a self coming into being via its self-perceptions . . . a narrator creating himself through his own narrative" (62). Indeed, there is a tendency to read into Molloy—as indeed into Malone and the Unnamable—a "universal" figure of self-creation. In his essay "Molloy's Silence" Georges Bataille frames *Molloy* as concerned with pure "ontology": "what *Molloy* reveals is not simply reality but reality in its pure state" (13); Molloy thus reveals the "essence of being" (14) as he creates himself through his narrative act. Commenting on Molloy's famous "saying is inventing" speech, however, Bataille posits Molloy/*Molloy* as going "beyond language," ignoring, I suppose, Gadamer's dictum "Being that can be understood is language." Bataille writes: "This is not a school's manifesto, not a manifesto at all but one expression, among others, of movements that go beyond any school and that want literature, finally, to make language into a facade, eroded by the wind and full of holes, that would possess the authority of ruins" (15).

It is clear that the critic regards the processes of subject and narrative creation as equal and arising out of a need or desire for fixity. In *Samuel Beckett: The Expressive Dilemma* Lawrence Miller posits Molloy's strategy as a "response to need: scraps of memory and observations are assembled in an attempt to create an other, and even himself" (70). Desire is also a theme of Eyal Amiran's *Wandering and Home:* "Molloy's clever solution to desire, then, is to find himself in a place without desire, but he never does" (106). Indeed, desire motivates all action in the trilogy, including Moran's own narrative, which has Molloy as, in Miller's nice phrase, its "ghostly *telos*" (84).

The relationship between Molloy and Moran is another major concern of critics. Most have a general feeling that Molloy and Moran are genetically or ontologically related. In *The Novels of Samuel Beckett,* H. Porter Abbott includes a chart detailing Molloy's and Moran's physical and narrative similarities but, wisely I feel, acknowledges the difficulty of establishing firmly any true links between the two in what he calls, perhaps pejoratively, "our obsession with unity" (99). Steven Connor, I think, provides the most theoretically sophisticated and satisfying account of the problematics of the relationship between Molloy and Moran. In *Samuel Beckett: Repetition, Theory, and Text* he formulates the issue as one of the relationship not between two individuals but two narratives. He details the "splitting of the self into simulacra" that arises at the point of narration: "Narration splits the subject into two, into a past self, the object of narration, and the present self who is doing the narrating. One might see the problem of narration as one of trying to enforce a bond of repeatability between these two selves" (52). This repeatability carries over into the relationship between the two halves of *Molloy.* Connor responds well to the temptation of reading Moran's narrative as preceding (temporally) Molloy's:

> For one thing, Moran's narrative doesn't actually precede Molloy's as we perhaps feel it should. This means that the moments of *deja vu* that we encounter in Moran's narrative—the concern with bicycles, the wicket-gate, the confusion between green and blue, the murdering of strangers etc.—are both originals *and* repetitions. They are originals at the level of *sjuzet*, in the narrative that we may construct to relate Moran to Molloy, but are repetitions at the level of *fabula*. (56)

This criticism, though sophisticated and important, still seems to me to be of a strictly formal type. It is rare to find a critic who looks beyond the hermetically sealed "boundaries" of the text to theorize affect. If Beckett's trilogy is marked by its own intense self-scrutiny, it seems a logical concomitant consideration would be that of the reader, who has somehow to arrive at a reading strategy for the self-conscious text. My suggestion here is founded in part on the sense that the Beckett oeuvre, especially as it reaches its maturity in the trilogy, is consciously fabricated with the reader in mind; indeed, as I have posited, the trilogy in one way may be understood to be "about" the "writerly" reader.

This is, of course, not to say that criticism fails absolutely to theorize affect. Abbott points to the trilogy, and *Molloy* in particular, as the beginning of Beckett's full application of "imitative form." His talk of Beckett's deliberate blocking of interpretation that "generat[es] in us the anxiety and enchantment of his narrators, who, like us, are struggling to order this material" (95) goes some way toward apprehending the affective impact of this text. Yet Abbott, strangely it seems to me, does not expend much energy in detailing the force of the *punctum* of *Molloy:* he is concerned more with detailing aspects of anxiety-producing form. Thus, although a gesture is made beyond the text, formal concerns are given more attention. The same criticism perhaps could be leveled at Kevin Dettmar, whose essay "The Figure in Beckett's Carpet: *Molloy*" makes a gesture toward theorizing the role of affect: "Molloy often confuses figurative and literal language. . . . But Molloy's hermeneutic situation is ours, and his confusion is our confusion as well" (76) but is primarily concerned with offering a taxonomy of Beckett's figural language: he does not, in short, theorize his own observations.

Paul Davies in *The Ideal Real* has a valuable chapter on *Molloy* in which the important questions regarding this text are at least posed. Davies, like Dettmar and Connor, is concerned with figurality and rhetoric, but he frames his analysis through the perception of actual readers, instead of merely observing rhetorical effect. Regarding Molloy's habit of saying a thing only to retract it, Davies writes: "But no sooner is the information given than it is taken away again. Why, it would be reasonable to ask, put it there in the first place? How can something be declared and denied at the same time?" (70). Davies's theorizing the response to this question—a question acknowledging the interrogative, thus affective, nature of the text—is one way of acknowledging the *punctum* of the text and the responsibility of reading.

The theoretical foundation of some of what follows builds on Wolfgang Iser's early work on Beckett in *The Implied Reader.* Iser's analysis of affect is crucial in that it theorizes affect and response while positing philosophical reasons behind Beckett's manipulation of the reader. On Molloy's self-contradictory rhetoric Iser writes: "The technique results in a total devaluation of language by accentuating the arbitrariness with which it is applied to the objects it seeks to grasp" (165). Iser, however, follows this observation with a consideration of a response to this rhetoric: "The text forces [the reader] to find his own way around, provoking questions to which he must supply his own answers" (175). Iser goes further to suggest a kind of proto-metahermeneutic as he posits the reader's reading of his own response, a reading mirroring that of the character: "The reader approaches the level of consciousness of Beckett's characters, and he only leaves it again when he seeks confirmation of his own experience and so restricts their 'play' by imposing a meaning on it. If he enters into the movement of the text, he will find it difficult to get out again, for he will find himself increasingly drawn into the exposure of the conditions that underlie his own judgement" (177). Iser's strength, it seems to me, lies in his theoretical foundations. His argument reaches its maximum density and impact in his purely theoretical musings on affect. Iser's work, however, approaches the level of a kind of literary philosophy, and thus a central paradox appears at the heart of his project: in detailing textual affect Iser often seems satisfied to leave the reader in the "abstract." Thus, although I find Iser's configurations of the reader/text relationship to be useful, an essential pragmatic element of textual analysis is missing from his work on Beckett. The result, I often find, is a reader sympathetic to but not really convinced of the force of Iser's argument. The following is, I hope, an attempt not to flesh out Iser's argument but to engage in close hermeneutical readings of a variety of scenes of "affect" in *Molloy*.

All I know is what the words know.
—Molloy

In this chapter I attempt through a variety of means to display the complex interrelationship between the thematics of subject, narrative-making, and the breakdown of epistemological categories. Each of the two narratives in *Molloy* has as a central concern the integrity of the writing subject, an integrity predicated on the stability of epistemological structures that would enable a self to "ground" itself, if only in discourse, and posit answers to those questions crucial for Beckett: "Where now? Who now? When now?" (*The Unnamable* 291). Yet the integrity of the logic of "subject" or "self and other"—categories configuring and seemingly underpinning the structure of the quest thematic of this novel as a whole—is one of the epistemologico-hermeneutical premises that *Molloy* actively deconstructs even as the characters themselves implicitly articulate the desire for the stability of a totalizing subject position: thus one of the responsibilities of the reader of the text is to trace how the thematic of the quest, with all its concomitant epistemological presuppositions, is undermined by what Moran, at a crucial moment, calls "the dispossession of self." Second, I wish to explore the text's creation and simultaneous decomposition of the specular, that is, reading, subject. *Molloy* is crucial in Beckett's oeuvre because it instantiates at the level of its binary structure an allegory of the text/reader relationship where Molloy "acts" as text to Moran's inexorable and hapless reading. Precisely as Beckett articulates his writing subject as reading subject (Moran)—thus thematizing or allegorizing hermeneutics—he imbricates his actual reader onto the same diegetic or semiotic plane that a reader-as-detective like Moran inhabits. Ultimately, then, these epistemological questions of location, subjectivity, and temporality—where? who? when?—become our own in a manner that simultaneously suggests the urgency of response and the ultimate impossibility of responding. The following cannot possibly do justice to the manifold complexities of *Molloy* but merely attempts to trace one thread of the thematics of the subject through its intimate relation to distinct "modes" of hermeneutical theory. I am concerned primarily with how the self realizes, and perhaps decomposes, itself *textually* and the concomitant apprehension of this process by the hermeneutical reader.

I take Emile Benveniste's writings on the subject, pronouns, and deixis as my starting point for a discussion of Molloy's narrative. In his essays "The Nature of Pronouns" and "Subjectivity in Language" Benveniste posits the role of the personal pronoun "I" as figuring, certainly presupposing, a "you": the sign "I" for Benveniste thus contains within itself the essential prefiguring of the subject-object relation, an essential epistemological category that, as we will see, *Molloy* and, indeed, the trilogy in toto, slowly dismantles. As is true for all of Beckett's works, Molloy's opening preamble is crucial for a number of reasons, not least for his insistent use of deixis and the consistently varying use of the pronouns "I" and "you." Deixis as grammatico-semiological figure, specifically here, the figures "here" "there" "now" work, as Benveniste suggests, to ground the writing subject/text in a temporal-spatial fixity (I emphasize the deixis I think crucial): "*I* am in my mother's room. It's *I* who live *there now*. I don't know how I got *there*. Perhaps in an ambulance, certainly a vehicle of some kind. *I* was helped. *I'd* never have got *there* alone" (7). The insistent "I" works to place the self in location ("my mother's room") and in "present" time (the five times repeated "now" in the opening paragraph). But we do notice a peculiarity as we trace along this level of deixis: Molloy works to establish himself in space and time, but his use of "there" instead of, presumably, "here" suggests a division, a distance—at least at the level of discourse—from this spatio-temporal "grounding." I stress this use of "there"—a figure pointing ostensibly "away" from the self—because of Molloy's insistent use of it (the French version of this opening shares some of these difficulties: "Je suis dans la chambre de ma mère. C'est moi qui y vis maintenant. Je ne sais pas comment j'y suis arrivé" [7]). Never once in this opening salvo is the deictic "here" used to ground Molloy spatio-temporally (although the French version has "Cet homme qui vient chaque semaine, c'est grâce à lui peut-être que je suis ici" [7] for "Perhaps I got there thanks to him"). Indeed, and this is important, Molloy uses "here" four times only to refer to the grounding of the self in the *textual*, rather than *physical*, moment. It is as if, perhaps, the textual takes precedence over the spatio-temporal:

> I began at the beginning, like an old ballocks, can you imagine that? Here's my beginning. Because they're keeping it apparently. I took a lot of trouble with it. Here it is. It gave me a lot of trouble. It was the beginning, do you understand? Whereas now it's nearly the end. Is what I do now any better? I don't know. That's beside the point. Here's my beginning. It must mean something, or they wouldn't keep it. Here it is. (8)

And, indeed, Molloy asserts overtly that the "now" of the writing is different than the "here" of the written: the "now" is "nearly the end" while the "here" of "here it is" or, more important, "here's my beginning" keeps Molloy perpetually in a state of "nostalgia," always seemingly glancing back on what has been. The effect here—an effect we are perhaps fully expecting—is a splitting into two "presents," the time of the narrator and the time of the narrated: both "presents," moreover, seem to bear equal authority, to exist in a perpetual balance.

This temporal "splitting" (or simultaneity) is echoed in Molloy's use of pronouns in the second paragraph, especially in the seeming interchangeability of "I" and "you"; thus the thematics of narrative time and of subject-making begin to correspond:

This time, then once more *I* think, then perhaps a last time, then *I* think it'll be over. All grows dim. A little more and *you'll* go blind. It's in the head. It doesn't work any more, it says, *I* don't work any more. *You* go dumb as well and sounds fade. The threshold scarcely crossed that's how it is. It's the head. It must have had enough. So that *you* say, *I'll* manage this time, then perhaps once more, then perhaps a last time, then nothing more. *You* are hard set to formulate this thought, for it is one, in a sense. (8)

I think this I/you opposition can be read in several ways. It suggests an essential split in Molloy as subject, a split echoing the temporal division of the self in narrative. Yet, following Benveniste for a moment, the I/you dialectic can be seen as a kind of interpenetrating "creation" of self, as the "I" always prefigures a "you": this "you" thus seems a logical concomitant self to inhabit the discrete temporal "zones" through which the narrative proceeds. If, as I figure it, this "you" is another aspect of Molloy, he "contains" the subject-object opposition in the same discursive space: this manipulation of the I/you dyad seems thus simultaneously to configure the subject-object category and to negate its "objective" epistemological status by interiorizing it.[1]

I wish, however, to emphasize the degree to which Molloy and *Molloy* involve the *actual* reader in the process of narration. This I/you dialectic—the I prefiguring a you—is a dialectic parallel in structure to the text-reader dialectical relationship. A narrative as narrative always presupposes and, if Iser and Jauss are to be believed, prescribes (inscribes) its reader. I think *Molloy* inscribes its reader in a number of ways, the most important being Moran, who is a literal reader of Molloy and thus a textual counterpart to the reader of *Molloy* (I will get to Moran in a moment). This "you," however, can also be read as an immediate appeal to, or grammatical "incorporation" of, the actual reader. Indeed, this is a point Ricoeur insists on in his essay "Appropriation," where he figures the "you" of a direct address to the reader as incorporating the reader into the text's "poetic universe." I do not wish to overburden or overread the "you-as-reader" notion here, only to suggest the inescapability *of* this "you": it must grammatically refer to the reader, just as, theoretically, it refers to the writer in his instance of discourse. I suggest this simply as a hint of larger degrees of specularity that will follow. Consider the following passage in Molloy's monologue and the semiological force of his "me": "But it is only since I have ceased to live that I think of these things. . . . It is in the tranquillity of decomposition that I remember the long confused emotion which was my life, and that I judge it, as it is said that God will judge me, and with no less impertinence. To decompose is to live too, I know, I know, don't torment me, but one sometimes forgets" (25). This "I know, I know, don't torment me" and his "to decompose is to live" are responses to questions the writer anticipates will be asked by the writer himself and by his own readers. Certainly we can read this passage as an instance of the mind in dialogue with itself, but it seems appropriate to this highly self-conscious narrator to see this as an anticipation of a response and an answer to a posed or self-created question. At the moment, in short, that Molloy poses the question, the reader is anticipated and created.

The temporal splitting that we noticed at the level of grammatico-semiological structures is again echoed in the peculiar and specific narrative/narratological positions in which Molloy and Moran find themselves: it is a position that unites and blends discrete temporalities, creating a discursive space described by Beckett as that of the "narrator/narrated."[2] It is a position that seemingly removes any ontological differences between inventing and remembering: *"Perhaps I'm inventing a little,* perhaps embellishing, but on the whole that's the way it was. They chew, swallow, then after a short pause effortlessly bring up the next mouthful. A neck muscle stirs and the jaws begin to grind again. *But perhaps I'm remembering things"* (8–9; emphasis added). The parallel grammatical structures here emphasize a link between two discrete temporalities and modes of self-creation. Invention and the act of remembrance are here equivalent, as Molloy often suggests as his narrative proceeds: several examples will illustrate the point:

> Dear bicycle, I shall not call you bike, you were green, like so many of your generation, I don't know why. It is a pleasure to meet it again. (16)

> I did not let it fall, no, but with a convulsive thrust of both my hands I threw it to the ground, where it smashed to smithereens, or against the wall, far from me, with all my strength. I will not tell what followed, for I am weary of this place, I want to go. (24)

> Yes, there is no denying it, any longer, it is not you who are dead, but all the others. So you get up and go to your mother, who thinks she is alive. That's my impression. But now I shall have to get myself out of this ditch. (27)

And Lousse? Must I describe her? I suppose so. Let's first bury the dog. (35)

Perhaps Moran characterizes this blend of temporalities most effectively: "For in describing this day I am once more he who suffered it" (122). The intimate relationship between remembrance and experience in *Molloy* will become a prominent theme, especially in *The Unnamable;* in *Molloy* it suggests a link between narrative—as a form of remembrance—and knowledge—as a form of experience. This is, however, a suggestion forwarded by Molloy himself, whose "Saying is inventing. Wrong, very rightly wrong" (32) suggests a link between saying and inventing (thus remembrance) but who always foregrounds the fact that as all experience is mediated by language—"All I know is what the words know"—any immediate experience of things seems always at a second's remove. Narrative thus inaugurates a particular epistemological crisis in Molloy. Molloy's "distance" from words places experience and, indeed, his sense of subjectivity, at a remove:

> I had been living so far from words so long, you understand, that it was enough for me to see my town, since we're talking of my town, to be unable, you understand. It's too difficult to say, for me. And even my sense of identity was wrapped in a namelessness often hard to penetrate, as we have just seen I think. . . . Yes, even then, when already all was fading, waves and particles, there could be no things but nameless things, no names but thingless names. . . . All I know is what the words know. (31)

Molloy's epistemological (subject) position here in the opening narrative can, I think, be read fruitfully through the lens of Gadamerian hermeneutics. The following attempts to make sense of the peculiar narrative difficulty of Molloy—his temporal splitting, his "subjective" splitting—in terms of Gadamer's notion of understanding as *dialogue*. In *Truth and Method* Gadamer posits understanding as the result or effect of a specifically linguistic exchange or dialogue: "Language is the medium in which substantive understanding and agreement take place between two people" (384): "It must be emphasised that language has its true being only in dialogue, in *coming to an understanding*. . . . But human language must be thought of as a special and unique life process since, in linguistic communication, 'world' is disclosed. Reaching an understanding in language places a subject matter before those communicating like a disputed object set between them" (446).

One way of reading Molloy's I/you split is therefore as an imaginary dialogue that attempts to reach understanding. The basic epistemological structure—the dialogical situation—is in place, and narrative itself thus begins to take on a specifically hermeneutical function. The difficulty for Molloy, as for his writerly counterparts, is that he is "alienated" from his own discourse. The situation here thus seemingly fits perfectly the Gadamerian understanding of the hermeneutical situation in which the object to be understood inhabits an alien "world" or discourse, although, as far as I can gather, Gadamer never overtly posits the hermeneutical subject *as object* (Molloy) being at a remove from his or her own discourse, despite the fact that for Gadamer understanding the object is always an understanding of the hermeneutical self. For Molloy to understand through and within an alienated medium removes the possibility of (self-)understanding at the outset because the basic hermeneutico-epistemological category of subject-object relations is undermined, knowingly or unknowingly, by Molloy at every turn: in fact, he configures himself as both subject and alienated object, I/you, narrator/narrated. Molloy reveals the depths of his (and our) hermeneutical difficulty when he pauses to offer his species of metahermeneutic:

> Oh I did not say it in such limpid language. And when I say I said, etc., all I mean is that I knew confusedly things were so, without knowing exactly what it was all about. And every time I say, I said this, or I said that, or speak of a voice saying, far away inside me, Molloy, and then a fine phrase more or less clear and simple, or find myself compelled to attribute to others intelligible words, or hear my own voice uttering to others more or less articulate sounds, I am merely complying with the convention that demands you either lie or hold your peace. For what really happened was quite different. (87–88)

Molloy concludes with "Molloy could stay, where he happened to be" (91), a sentence containing a maximum compression of a variety of epistemological "themes": he places himself at a third person's remove and spatially in a location ill-defined but thematically perfectly suited to the (pseudo) quest that will follow in Moran's narrative. Yet I think the major semiotic resonance here at the conclusion is sounded in the above-quoted "For what really happened was quite different"; here Molloy again complies with the Beckettian convention that demands you say one thing only to retract it. The effect, an effect "worked out" in *Mercier and Camier*, undermines any "authority" the preceding may have had and works again to remind the reader the degree to which the making of narrative-as-subject in Beckett is a protean, ultimately ethereal—ultimately textual—event: if a subject appears, he can as easily disappear, leaving the reader, at times incorporated into the text, to wonder what she or he saw and how to read it.

I have traced the subject position of Molloy thus far to suggest two things. First, he is unable to locate himself firmly in space or in time. Second, as one alienated from his own discourse, he admits the impossibility of reaching an understanding of his present situation, of answering that basic hermeneutical question: "How does it stand toward me?" Molloy's epistemological crisis is the crisis of narrative or discourse; Molloy cannot "locate" himself even in his own discursive productions. Molloy is twice lost, as it were. The irony in place here—and *Molloy* is constructed in the logic of the ironic displacement of horizons of expectations—is that the ultimate object of the hermeneutical quest of Moran (and reader), Molloy, cannot even be posited: the very terms of the "quest" are confounded a priori as the end of the quest cannot even be "thought" by the pursuer and, most radically, by the pursued.

And yet the second part of *Molloy* will thematize the reader and work to present the hermeneutical pursuit of what cannot be thought or what exists only as a kind of projection of the pursuing subject. The second part of *Molloy* interiorizes the preceding narrative in order to place it within a coherent and cohering frame even as the logic of the first admits of the ultimate futility of doing so. In Moran's narrative Beckett continues to explore the limits of hermeneutical understanding based on imperfect or unclear (self-)knowledge. The irony suggested by Beckett in Moran's narrative is that epistemological or narrative frames can cohere only if the hermeneutical subject (the reading subject) can maintain a firm spatiotemporal grasp on "reality." We will find that the subject in *Molloy* is always in disintegrative crisis and that Moran's quest is almost by definition always failing. The interest for the hermeneutical reader of Moran's narrative thus is not whether Moran will "find" Molloy (the idea of discovery in Beckett being fraught with a myriad of epistemological crises) but in *how* Beckett consigns his reader(s) to epistemological crisis and how this is complicated by the working out of the discourse of hermeneutic specularity.

> I am paid to seek.
> —Moran

Most critics, as I have suggested, posit or intuit a genetic if not ontological link between Molloy and Moran. In the following I am interested not so much in pursuing this "essential" relationship; rather I will posit a hermeneutical ground on and through which a relationship is articulated. I take as a basic or primary fact that Moran is in pursuit of Molloy and that this pursuit is a specific aspect of an overarching hermeneutical quest: I suggest, for instance, Moran's narrative as being in part a "reading" of Molloy's. This section is concerned with framing Moran's quest specifically in hermeneutical terms positing, ultimately, Moran as Beckett's first fully formed specular reader.

It is important, I think, to notice the seeming sharp contrast in the tone and "syntax" of the discourse of Moran's narrative to that of Molloy. Moran's narrative opens with an overtly confident tone—a tone structured, perhaps, on a kind of scientific exactitude. Where Molloy's opening paragraph articulates itself on a dialectic of deictic instability, Moran's is full of bluff and self-confidence. He establishes a setting and, crucially, an identity: he is able to name himself immediately, as opposed to Molloy, who remembers (or "remembered") his name only well into his narrative; Moran writes:

> It is midnight. The rain is beating on the windows. I am calm. All is sleeping. Nevertheless I get up and go to my desk. I can't sleep. My lamp sheds a soft and steady light. I have trimmed it. It will last till morning. I hear the eagle-owl. What a terrible battle-cry! Once I listened to it unmoved. My son is sleeping. Let him sleep. The night will come when he too, unable to sleep, will get up and go to his desk. I shall be forgotten.
>
> My report will be long. Perhaps I shall not finish it. My name is Moran, Jacques. That is the name I am known by. I am done for. My son too. All unsuspecting. He must think he's on the threshold of life, of real life. He's right there. His name is Jacques, like mine. This cannot lead to confusion. (92)

The reader may feel compelled into a different position from that assumed when reading Molloy's narrative. The seeming confidence of Moran places the reader in a posture not immediately concerned with interrogating the basic signposts of either narrative or narrative subject position: in short, there seems at the outset to be little "writerly" work to be done. But this is of course only an immediate illusion, for Moran occupies a space of pure unknowing: his ontological position is as unsure and tenuous as Molloy's. The difference immediately apparent to the reader is that Moran seems able to frame his position precisely *as* a position of ignorance. Thus Moran's relationship to Youdi and his messenger Gaber is unclear; the force impelling the quest is ill-defined; the agents communicate in a code unreadable by Moran; indeed, as he says, and will say again, "All this is not very clear" (107).

Moran's relationship to Molloy (or Mollose?) is therefore a priori ill-defined and can be read at least from one perspective as an articulation of a specifically hermeneutical type of desire. I suggest this paradigm keeping in mind the structural arrangement of *Molloy*, which has Moran's narrative following Molloy's sequentially. Positing Molloy as hermeneutical object of Moran allows us perhaps to tease out a structural similarity between the relationship of Moran to Molloy and the reader/text hermeneutical relationship, or perhaps as an emphatic structural echo of the I/you relation we noticed in Molloy's narrative. And, indeed, if we accept the relationship in hermeneutical terms, some of Moran's more cryptic musings, musings that are usually read as "identifying" Moran as Molloy, begin to make some sense. Consider the following in terms of the Heideggerian *Vorgriff* or the Gadamerian "prejudice":

> Molloy, or Mollose, was no stranger to me. If I had had colleagues, I might have suspected I had spoken of him to them, as of one destined to occupy us, sooner or later. But I had no colleagues and knew nothing of the circumstances in which I had learnt of his existence. *Perhaps I had invented him, I mean found him ready made in my head.* . . . *For who could have spoken to me of Molloy if not myself and to whom if not to myself could I have spoken of him?* (111–12; emphasis added)

Most critics see in these lines a suggestion of Moran and Molloy's genetic self-identity. For my purposes it does not matter if Moran and Molloy are one and the same; what matters is that one is in hermeneutical pursuit of the other: "Between the Molloy I stalked within me thus and the true Molloy, after whom I was so soon to be in full cry, over hill and dale, the resemblance cannot have been great" (115). It is here a question not so much of genetic identity, or self-identity, but rather of priority. From a hermeneutical perspective, at least as formulated by Gadamer, a true hermeneutical encounter—and I am suggesting Moran and Molloy's relationship is fundamentally a hermeneutical one—blurs the question of ontological simultaneity or priority. The two members of the hermeneutical dialogue or dialectic will meet, but the essence of the encounter takes place "in between" the interlocutors. More important, however, and the subjective transformation of Moran over the course of the novel confirms this, the hermeneutical encounter is actively transformational: it is, as Gadamer puts it, a "communion in which we do not remain what we were" (379).

And at the moment we perceive the hermeneutical nature of Moran's quest, we can begin to unravel the specular elements of his narrative (hermeneutical) position. Because Moran's quest blends with the reader's desire for knowledge, however rudimentary, of Molloy, Moran begins to act in a specular manner: his quest is ours, ours is his. Specularity thus bridges—or, perhaps more precisely, threatens to bridge—the "ontological" gap between reader and text in a way that accents or limns the *hermeneutical* nature of the textual experience: specularity always thematizes hermeneutical desire.

I wish to be clear here about what I mean by the discourse of specularity: I do not mean simply that we "identify" with a certain character, that is, sympathize or empathize with him or her in the space of the textual encounter. I mean that, as far as it is possible in the economy of the text/reader relationship, the reader is obliged to assume a hermeneutical position close if not identical to that of the textual reader, in this case, Moran. The discourse of specularity as employed by Beckett always involves a degree of violation of the specular reader or readers. What is crucial to notice about Beckett's manipulation of this specular reader's "stand in," or simulacrum, is that he or she always undergoes some sort of psychic if not physical disintegration, that is, a particularly radical form of "hermeneutical transformation." The dialectic of reading Beckett through his specular reader is thus one of hermeneutic identification and violation. My sense here is that Beckett succeeds in imbricating or articulating his reader into the text and forces him or her via the specular reader into a space where the subject, or subjectivity, is utterly negated: if, as I contend, the reader assumes the role of specular reader, his readerly subject position becomes tenuous as it too is decomposed. In Lacanian terms, this specular relationship functions within the Imaginary realm: I identify with another (reader) in some ways to attempt a fuller understanding of my own position. But as Lacan notices—and what is crucial here—is that this process of identification, this hermeneutic Imaginary, involves not a little discomfort. As the child in the mirror phase identifies with somebody outside of him or herself, she or he notices that the blurring of identity comes at a cost: if the body outside the self feels pain so does the self. My exploration of the Imaginary hermeneutic suggests that our identification with the specular reader too comes at a price: as the specular reader is decomposed, our position of secure distance is radically called into question.

Specularity, though not termed as such, is a point insisted on in the hermeneutics of both Gadamer and Ricoeur; I have previously figured Gadamer's notion of *phronesis* (practical judgment as action) as an obligation thrust onto the reader. In a specifically hermeneutic reading of a text, in this case *Molloy*, the analogical or specular relation between reader and character (Moran) is in place: I posit this relation as conferring—a word first used in this book in my reading of *Watt*—an obligatory role onto the reader, a role that transforms or translates the reader's position or posture of "distance" to one of absolute (and ultimately ethical) proximity "to" the text. The structure of specularity in its precise relation to the reader of the text thus begins to unbalance the reader-as-subject/text-as-object relationship in a way that, first, echoes the thematics of the decomposition of the category of subject/object; second, specularity demands that the reader reconfigure what may be the traditional epistemological stance of reader maintaining the coherence of self, despite or even because of the effects of "appropriation," in relation to coherence of text. This transformational role is noted by Ricoeur in his essay "Hermeneutics and the Critique of Ideology":

> To understand is not to project oneself into the text but to expose oneself to it; it is to receive a self enlarged by the appropriation of the proposed worlds which interpretation unfolds. In sum, it is the matter of the text which gives the reader his dimension of subjectivity; understanding is thus no longer a constitution of which the subject possesses the key. Pressing the suggestion to the end, we must say that the subjectivity of the reader is no less held in suspense, no less potentialised, than the very world which the text unfolds. In other words, if fiction is a fundamental dimension of the reference of the text, it is equally a fundamental dimension of the subjectivity of the reader: in reading, I "unrealize myself." Reading introduces me to imaginative variations of the *ego*. (94)

Although I agree with Ricoeur about the transformational relationship of subject to text, I wish to emphasize the degree to which in a reading of Beckett "appropriation"—the reader's appropriation of the text's "world"—is always a "conferred" appropriation. The reader of *Molloy*, I posit, has very little choice about undergoing a subjective transformation via the specular subject: the subject position is conferred onto the reader via the economy of the hermeneutical/specular subject-reader relationship.

Beckett sets up the decomposition or transformation of the hermeneutical and specular subject in a series of incremental steps; it begins at the outset as the reading subject (Moran) is placed within a hermeneutical space without any firm ontological context or signposts: his "thrownness," to borrow from Heidegger, mirrors that of the reader, who has only the noncontext of Moran to orient his or her own reading. Beckett proceeds delicately to strip away the illusion of firm subjectivity ("My name is Moran, Jacques") by again playing with the first and third person dialectic so pronounced in Molloy's own narrative: "For where Molloy could not be, nor Moran either for that matter, there Moran could bend over Molloy" (111); or again:

> It was then the unheard of sight was to be seen of Moran making ready to go without knowing where he was going, having consulted neither map nor timetable, considered neither itinerary nor halts, heedless of the weather outlook, with only the vaguest notion of the outfit he would need, the time the expedition was likely to take, the money he would require and even the very nature of the work to be done and consequently the means to be employed. And yet there I was whistling away. (124)

> And it was not so much Moran as another, in the secret of Moran's sensations exclusively, who said, No change, Moran, no change. This may seem impossible. I went into the copse to cut myself a stick. (147)

And indeed, there is a moment in the text that acts as a perfect emblem of this narrative and subjective decomposition. It is an extraordinarily complex, because extraordinarily resonant, *mise-en-abyme* of the entire thematics of quest-narrative-subject/reader-text relationship. Moran is alone in what he calls "Molloy country" (133) after having sent his son off to buy a bike:

> I surrendered myself to the beauties of the scene, I gazed at the trees, the fields, the sky, the birds, and I listened attentively to the sounds, faint and clear, borne to me on the air. For an instant I fancied I heard the silence mentioned, if I am not mistaken, above. Stretched out in the shelter, I brooded on the undertaking in which I was embarked. I tried again to remember what I was to do with Molloy, when I

found him. I dragged myself down to the stream. I lay down and
looked at my reflection, then I washed my face and hands. I waited
for my image to come back, I watched it as it trembled towards an
ever increasing likeness. Now and then a drop, falling from my face,
shattered it again. (145)

The passage immediately—and ironically—evokes Narcissus attempting to embrace his own likeness and failing and dying. The Narcissus myth should be read as an exploration of the failure to differentiate self from other and the dangers of this failure. What I think is crucial about the passage is the implicit causal relationship between the act of remembrance—more precisely, the attempted act of remembrance—and the act of self-reflection: there seems to be a definite link between Moran's attempt to remember what to do with Molloy and the act of looking at himself in the stream, as if perhaps the clues to the means of action were written in Moran's own face. The clues, however, if they are in place, are inscrutable; moreover, Moran's own image of self, which may provide the means of action, is constructed in a balance of dissipation and coherence. Moran, unlike Narcissus, never mistakes his "image" for an other; but on a metaphoric level, his image of self seems always on the *verge* of merging into a resemblance of himself (becoming): "it trembled towards an ever increasing likeness" (145). The coherence of self is a crucial element in "tracking" Molloy, as Molloy somehow inheres in Moran. But his image of self is "shattered" (145) as the water breaks the surface of the stream. The shattering of Moran's image of self here, as it is placed in a fairly resonant mythic context and as it thematizes the notions of self, self-identity, and dissipation, thus carries a huge semiotic weight into the totality of the novel. Moran's sense of self, as it is mirrored in the water—and the water becomes for me an emblem of textuality—is bound by the unsynthesizable dialectic of communion and loss.

This passage in fact inaugurates a series of encounters between Moran, various simulacra of himself, and "abysmal" specular (that is, [self-]reflecting) structures, all of which serve to highlight what Moran himself calls his "great inward metamorphoses" (163). The second specular vision in water occurs soon after the one described above and explicitly thematizes the loss of both the sense of subjectivity crucial for the carrying out of the hermeneutic quest, and, more important, the loss of a "directed" hermeneutic desire:

And then I saw a little globe swaying up slowly from the depths,
through the quiet water, smooth at first, and scarcely paler than its

escorting ripples, then little by little a face, with holes for the eyes and mouth and other wounds, and nothing to show if it was a man's face or a woman's face, a young face or an old face, or if its calm too was not an effect of the water trembling between it and the light. But I confess I attended but absently to these poor figures, in which I suppose my sense of disaster sought to contain itself. And that I did not labour at them more diligently was a further index of the great changes I had suffered and of my growing resignation to being dispossessed of self. (148–49)

Following this vision, which seems to portend something—and we notice the divide again in Moran's reading of this figural image, between sensing a disastrous significance and a sense of absolute dispossession—and which most clearly articulates Moran's fractured subject position, both hermeneutic desire is lost and the self begins to find vague simulacra in the external world; it is as if as the sense of self is lost, it sets up echoes of itself shimmering about Moran; it is a perfect visual metaphor for the dissolution and dissipation of the self. Moran's encounter with the man in the woods, whose face, Moran says, "I regret to say vaguely resembled my own" (151), compels an oddly disproportionate emotional response, as if, having become resigned to the dispossession of self, the mirror of the man's face is too painful for Moran to bear; and indeed, following his killing of the man Moran comments blithely: "he no longer resembled me" (151).

Moran's dispossession of self, which I figure as heralding the loss of the hermeneutic compulsion, makes some sense of the rambling lists of questions Moran proceeds to ask himself (154, 166–67). One way of reading the rhetorical effect of these lists is as the effect of a kind of diffused or sublimated hermeneutic desire; where first the desire was to find Molloy, here the questions in the initial list do not concern Molloy at all; moreover, the questions themselves defy the logic of answerability even at the moment of asking: "But while looking for the answer, or the answers, to a given question, I found the answer, or the answers, to a question I had already asked myself in vain, in the sense that I had not been able to answer it, or I found another question, or other questions, demanding in their turn an immediate answer" (154). The second and third lists contain for me the maximum compression of Moran's hermeneutical confusion. The questions of esoteric religious significance cannot, I think, be easily harmonized with the tenor of Moran's narrative but seem rather to contain a refraction of the hermeneutic quest: hermeneutic desire is transposed—as the logic of the quest structure, with its integral elements of pursuing subject and pursued object, is decomposed—onto an entirely irrelevant semiotic plane. In fact, the final list, which begins with questions dealing with the nature of the quest and ends with asking the name of an obscure martyr, contains in miniature the hermeneutical movement of Moran's total narrative as it mirrors the gradual movement away from "directedness" or significance (or the possibility of significance) that is traced by Moran himself. It seems finally that Moran cannot end his narrative with anything else but specular and structural simulacra of his own abject position as dispossessed self.

And thus the reader, who wishes to read Molloy through Moran—or, more precisely, is seduced into believing in the possibility of reading Molloy through Moran—is placed in a difficult narratological or semiological "zone" where the reading lens, as it were, becomes diffused and darkened. Moran, and Molloy through him, becomes the reader's own "dim man," "dim of face and dim of body, because of the dark" (150). Moran, as hermeneutical subject, thus is in a fairly ineluctable state of subjective decline as his narrative proceeds. And as the subject of his quest becomes more and more ill-defined ("What it was all about I haven't the slightest idea" [113]) and the telos or end of the quest (or narrative) recedes into perpetual dimness ("What was I looking for exactly? It is hard to say" [126]): "Stories, stories. I have not been able to tell this one" (137), the narrator as subject—and specular reader—is slowly dismantled.

Thus in some fashion the final paragraph of Moran's narrative contains the maximum compression of aporia in *Molloy*. Where in a typical detective procedural we expect the questions posed at the outset to be incrementally answered as the narrative proceeds and concludes, Moran's narrative winds itself down into incoherence and contradiction:

> I have spoken of a voice telling me things. I was getting to know it better now, to understand what it wanted. It did not use the words that Moran had been taught when he was little and that he in his turn had taught to his little one. So that at first I did not know what it wanted. But in the end I understood this language. I understood it, I understood it, all wrong perhaps. This is not what matters. It told me to write the report. Does this mean I am freer now than I was? I do not know. I shall learn. Then I went back into the house and wrote, It is midnight. The rain is beating on the windows. It was not midnight. It was not raining. (175–76)

Moran's final words circle back on the entire report and work to suggest a negation of the truth value of the entire narrative by denying the truth of the opening sentences, "It is midnight. The rain is beating on the windows" (92). The entire narrative is thus "contained" within a framework the first premises of which are incrementally revealed as untenable. This gesture—typical enough in Beckett—leaves the reader in a difficult but by now familiar position, again wondering, "By what token shall we know the truth?" The final passage, moreover, involves a strange manipulation, or dislocation, of temporal sequence as it articulates itself in the past tense problematizing the present tense of the opening "It is midnight. The rain is beating on the windows." The problem for the reader thus is in determining the *present* moment of writing and self-creation: when does/did Moran write the report? We have a narrative that begins in the present tense, ends in the present—"Does this mean I am freer *now* than I was?"— but casts an eye retrospectively back on what *was* written as if excluding the possibility of narrative progression in traditional terms of telos: the moment of writing is thus endlessly "present," if not tautological. The result of Moran's endless present is, I think, to suggest a kind of self-imprisonment in a self-imprisoning narrative, bound always in a narrative moment that denies the entire economy of "progression." Yet the fact remains that hermeneutic desire, even as it is diffused in these final pages of the narrative, is still present, just as the narrative as a whole is still present and has been brought into existence by a writing self in search of *something*. Beckett's characters are formed in the space between two contradictory impulses: the desire for self-abnegation and the desire to "know." It is the inexorable articulation of this aporetic division that constitutes the central thematic impulse of Moran's narrative.

Molloy resonates on at least three interrelated levels, all of which collapse the notion of the integrity of the subject under intense epistemological crisis. First, as a detective procedural, the text decomposes its generic inheritance by collapsing the structure or logic of pursuit by negating the notions of "subject of quest" and "object of quest." There is thus a double crisis of subject where the pursuing subject (Moran) cannot define the ends of the quest even as he cannot define the *moment* of his pursuit. Second, a reading of *Molloy* as an allegory of the hermeneutical encounter collapses under the pressure of attempting to define and delimit the "horizon" or "world" of both reader (Moran) and text (Molloy): both horizons are so ill-defined that no "dialogue" can ever take place. Third,

Molloy works to suggest the absolute decomposition of the category of "self and other," or subject and object, the basic premise, that is, of both hermeneutics and epistemology: the economy of this text works to dismantle the basic notion of subject/object relations in a way that removes the possibility of even conceiving the logic of the opposition. Both the narratives of Molloy and Moran, as they seem to divide the narrating subject into discrete selves inhabiting discrete temporalities, suggest an essential division of the self harboring the illusion that it exists as both subject and object, as both writing subject and object of discourse: the point I am making here is that the division of self is only a *discursive* division of the self or subject, not the creation of an epistemologically sound "object," or objective, category. Moreover, because the writing subject cannot locate himself discursively as subject, the entire logic of subject presupposing object—I presupposing you, Moran being "able" to pursue Molloy—is dismantled even as the desire for the efficacy of the structure is implicitly articulated. The question thus that we need to explore in *Malone Dies* and *The Unnamable*—texts themselves thematizing epistemologico-hermeneutical crises—is whether the removal of the category of subject-object leaves the writing (or is it speaking?) subject in discursive solipsism or whether the notion of solipsism, one seemingly perfectly applicable to the Unnamable's situation, for instance, requires a perceiving subject aware of himself *as* subject.

4

Malone Dies

> There I am back at my old aporetics.
> —Malone

This chapter continues the exploration of the instantiation of "self" in text. In *Malone Dies* Beckett remains concerned with the thematic of the aporetic division of self in the textual object, and here again he explicitly foregrounds the "fabrication" of text through the narrative constructions of Malone: "While waiting," says Malone, "I shall tell myself stories" (180). And indeed, it is the text's own mode of self-reflexive awareness that interests many readers of *Malone Dies*. I examine the hermeneutical significance of two instances of self-reflexivity in the novel. The first is Malone's habit of offering commentary on the narratives he tells. This self-reflexive gesture—a gesture consciously aware of itself *as* metanarrative—figures Malone as the originary critic of his own work. The second self-reflexive gesture is the related thematic of the "game" or "play." Malone categorizes his stories as "play," and I will suggest that a full understanding of how play is articulated in this text can come about only if the topos of play is read back into its hermeneutical contexts as, for instance, formulated by Gadamer and Ricoeur.

In *Homo Ludens*, a text crucial to both Gadamer and Ricoeur in their hermeneutical configurations of play, Johan Huizinga posits play as a gesture specifically related to the desire for order; indeed, for Huizinga play "*is* order" (29). I argue here that the totality of Malone's narrative, as it delimits the time remaining in Malone's life, expresses precisely this desire for order and thus can be understood as an articulation of play. But as both Gadamer and Ricoeur suggest, "play"—as it articulates itself within the semiology of the aesthetic object: here Malone's own stories and the totality of *Malone Dies*—will constitute the subjectivity of reader/writer (Malone is both) within a space where subjectivity itself, that is, self-conscious awareness of "selfhood," is "playfully" placed under erasure. Indeed, in strict hermeneutical terms, the concept and operation of play explicitly negate the subject's awareness of self. Taken together thus, Malone's texts and concomitant metatext (his commentaries) designate two aporetic "roles" for the writing subject. On the one hand, Malone's stories express a desire for "playful" subjective erasure; on the other, the metatext exposes a perverse and acutely painful awareness of the impossibility of achieving this kind of nullification in text, of the impossibility of writing the moment of selflessness (nonbeing). Malone discovers in this text the intimate connection between Being and (the) language (of play). Language simultaneously constitutes Being and acts to disfigure the understanding of self "in" language: understanding of Being, in short, is mediated by that which constitutes Being a priori. Malone's constant irruption into metanarrative, therefore, operates to signify the ineluctable process of self-scrutiny even as the priority of the writing subject is acknowledged: "And I call that playing. I wonder if I am not talking yet again about myself" (189). The difficulty here for Malone is not, as is the case for Molloy and Moran, the maintenance of the coherence of the writing subject but the maintenance of the coherence—the "objective" status—of the textual product, text that serves as both screen, onto which particular desires are projected, and mirror, reflecting back and thereby consolidating (or disfiguring) those desires. The central aporia of this text thus arises as Malone attempts to maintain the discrete economy of the space of play beside the self-conscious semiological zone of the metanarrative, indeed, in how the text defines and divides itself along two opposing and seemingly irreconcilable conceptions of "being" in play.

The critical community recognizes the thematic, if not hermeneutical, significance of the game and "playing" in *Malone Dies*. Leo Bersani in "Beckett and the End of Literature" notes the connection between play and Malone's intense self-awareness as teller of stories: "What destroys the resolution of the early pages [that is, the resolution to tell stories] is Malone's inability to talk about anything but himself (to be able to do that would be 'to play')" (63). In "Fiction, Myth, and Identity in Samuel Beckett's Novel Trilogy," Leslie Hill notes that Malone's "oscillation between fiction and interjection [is] thematized by Malone as a 'jeu'" (92). Hill's conception of the logic of play is, however, completely at odds with a hermeneutical reading of play: the oscillation he notes is itself the mark precisely of the inability to achieve the state of play. In "The Self-Multiplying Narrators of *Molloy, Malone Dies,* and *The Unnamable,*" Charlotte Renner notes merely that "by 'playing,' Malone hopes to pass the time remaining until his impending death" (104), a statement, though perhaps true in the narrowest of senses, that does nothing to acknowledge the problematics of defining Malone's activities *as* play or to acknowledge the manifold complexities of the very notion of play even separated from the context of Beckett's own work; in Renner's reading one gets the sense of the degree to which Beckett critics often allow the text unproblematically to dictate the terms and parameters of their own reading. Wolfgang Iser in his chapter "Subjectivity as the Autogenous Cancellation of Its Own Manifestation" in *The Implied Reader* notes more usefully that "the stories are 'play' insofar as they are not devised for the sake of an ultimate meaning but only for meanings that will ward off the void" (75); the "diversion" of the story allows Malone to go "beyond his known self" (75).

My difficulties with these critical readings of Malone's "play" are based on the sense that the critic either merely thematizes (describes) the function of play or does not push thematization far enough "into" the text. Several critics (Iser, Bersani), for instance, note the relationship between the subject positions of Malone as writer and narrator and his "playing" but do not note, and this is strange from a critic of Iser's hermeneutic inheritance, the importance—for the reader, for Malone—of Malone's *inability* (or is it unwillingness?) to maintain the self under erasure. Moreover, and this is a crucial contention of this chapter, Malone's irruption into metanarrative always will inaugurate the reader's own awareness of text and, more specifically, his or her relation to text as reader: thus Malone's intense self-awareness must always have as a necessary and inescapable concomitant the reader's own awareness of self as reader (of reader).

Malone categorizes his activity as "play" in the second paragraph of his narrative:

> This time I know where I am going, it is no longer the ancient night, the recent night. Now it is a game, I am going to play. I never knew how to play, till now. I longed to, but I knew it was impossible. . . . From now on it will be different. I shall never do anything any more from now on but play. No, I must not begin with an exaggeration. But I shall play a great part of the time, from now on, the greater part, if I can. But perhaps I shall not succeed any better than hitherto. Perhaps as hitherto I shall find myself abandoned, in the dark, without anything to play with. Then I shall play with myself. To have been able to conceive such a plan is encouraging. (180)

For Malone his playing will take the form of storytelling, a way, as most critics note, of passing the time. The crucial thing for my purposes here is to keep foregrounded the fact that Malone makes every effort to keep the stories from being "about" himself: the narratives thus have as "purpose," in the loose sense of the word, a kind of self-forgetfulness.[1] Play, even as Malone understands it—and I posit his understanding as hermeneutical at its base—involves, as Gadamer posits in *Truth and Method,* two important interrelated components:

> Play clearly represents an order in which the to-and-fro motion of play follows of itself. It is part of play that the movement is not only without goal or purpose but also without effort. It happens, as it were, by itself. (104–5)

> In playing, all those purposive relations that determine active and caring existence have not simply disappeared, but are curiously suspended. The player himself knows that play is only play and that it exists in a world determined by the seriousness of purposes. But he does not know this in such a way that, as a player, he actually *intends* this relation to seriousness. *Play fulfills its purpose only if the player loses himself in play.* (102)[2]

And yet Malone interrupts the flow of his narrative with "What tedium. And I call that playing. I wonder if I am not talking yet again about myself. Shall I be incapable, to the end, of lying on any other subject?" (189). At best Malone's first narrative is a stuttering affair: "Sapo had no friends—no that won't do" (189); "He boxed and wrestled well, was fleet of foot, sneered at his teachers and sometimes even gave them impertinent answers. Fleet of foot? Well well" (189); "Sapo loved nature, took an interest—This is awful" (191). The question we might ask here is, Does what Malone produces, and his stand toward it, constitute "being" in the game? (Is it even appropriate, given Gadamer's notion of play being without "goal or purpose," to call a narrative a game or play at all?) The answers to these questions will, I think, determine the nature of Malone's position as narrator and will enable us to read in a more fruitful way the self-reflexive, metanarrative comments by Malone as his narratives proceed.

A response to these questions requires the reader of *Malone Dies* to take into account the movement of Malone's narrative as a sequential structuration. I use the word "sequence" to account for the processual structure of the stories that begins with the stuttering narrative of Sapo and ends with Lemuel's slaughter at the outing of the mental patients. Primarily because the structure of Malone's narrative is conceived beforehand—"I think I shall be able to tell myself four stories, each one on a different theme" (181)—the reader expects, perhaps naively, some structure of order, if not meaning, to appear as the stories progress and, most important, as they conclude. The logic of sequence thus requires that Malone's final narrative resonate with a certain amount of *significance*. And, indeed, some critics see the final narrative as having that semio-narratological resonance; Leo Bersani, for instance, characterizes the episode of Lemuel's slaughter as a dramatization of Malone's own dying: he thus confers onto this final text an implicit teleological significance and resonance. A teleological reading of structuration founders, however, on its underestimation and denial of the cumulative rhetorical effect of Malone's intense self-consciousness and metanarrative intrusions. These narratives are all presented as "invented," consciously portrayed as constructed text, even as tedious text. As such, a homogenization of significance—a semiological "flattening"—takes place over the course of the presentation of the narratives. This is an effect noted by Maurice Blanchot in his essay "Where Now? Who Now?" Blanchot maintains that Malone's stories themselves "do not signify" (25) because the reader always expects something else to confer significance onto the textual productions. In fact, all semiological acts in Malone's narrative are related back to one source: Malone, who himself categorizes the narratives thus: "While waiting I shall tell myself stories, if I can. They will not be the same kind of stories as hitherto, that is all. They will be neither beautiful nor ugly, they will be calm, there will be no ugliness or beauty or fever in them any more, they will be almost lifeless, like the teller" (180). Even in those moments in the text where Malone achieves what appears to be the coherence of transparent narrative (if only momentarily) his previous categorizations of his own textual productions frame what appears free of the self-conscious narrator *as* only story, only as product unable to refer beyond the subjective boundaries of the obsessive narrator; all narrative productions here are a posteriori coded back to Malone: the texts Malone produces elaborate in their semiological neutering the erasure of the transparent narrative act.

Because there is no overriding teleological structure in place as *Malone Dies* proceeds and concludes, we may be tempted to harmonize the "disinterested" narrative structure of the text with Gadamer's sense that the game sees the suspension of "purposive relations": the stories of Malone thus seem to correspond with one aspect of the hermeneutical notion of play. But this is only a reading of *Malone Dies* along the axis of structuration: at the level of the semiology of the metanarrative—and my argument above is intended to suggest that metanarrative is inescapable in all of Malone's semiological productions—the totality of *Malone Dies* seems always to resist the erasure of subjectivity and thus to resist the logic of play.

And it is as we begin to read the semiology of the metanarrative as play that the concomitant issue of specularity again arises. Indeed, in Malone's irruptive commentary we have an articulation of what I have called a metahermeneutic, precisely, a hermeneutic of a hermeneutic, an interpretation of narrative in which the interpretive stance of reader—and Malone is the originary reader of his narratives—is framed by a particular epistemological position. Malone makes it clear that his narratives express the desire for an "ordering" of the time left to him. More important, his present occupation is explicitly framed in terms of self-"knowledge": "And I even feel a strange desire come over me, the desire to know what I am doing, and why" (194); "All I want now is to make a last effort to understand" (199). Malone emphatically links his writing to the process of coming to an understanding: "My little finger glides before my pencil across the page and gives warning, falling over the edge, that the end of the line is near. But in the other direction, I mean of course vertically, I have nothing to guide me. I did not want to write, but I had to resign myself to it in the end. It is in order to know where I have got to, where he has got to" (207). Malone figures the textual product as a sort of mirror consolidating his particular epistemological desires: the production of text as "play" has a specific ordering purpose. Malone's articulation of the function of his text thus harmonizes with Huizinga's notion of the existential-aesthetic effect of the play function:

> Inside the play-ground an absolute and peculiar order reigns. Here we come across another, very positive feature of play: it creates order, *is* order. Into an imperfect world and into the confusion of life it brings a temporary, a limited perfection. Play demands order absolute and supreme. The least deviation from it "spoils the game," robs it of its character, and makes it worthless. The profound affinity between play and order is perhaps the reason why play, as we noted in passing, seems to lie to such a large extent in the field of aesthetics. ... It may be that this aesthetic factor is identical with the impulse to create orderly form, which animates play in all its aspects. (29)

Yet despite Malone's explicit articulation of epistemological desire, the narratives he tells seem always to exceed his own interpretive grasp: if the interpretive/hermeneutic act precedes or is simultaneous to epistemological understanding or "grounding," the narratives Malone tells will consistently resist his own "fore-conceptions" of them. Malone's own act of reading cannot locate or fix understanding in the textual product: "I have tried to reflect on the beginning of my story. There are things I do not understand. But nothing to signify" (189). Plot events seem just out of his authorial control: "But Sapo was not expelled, either then or later. I must try and discover, when I have time to think about it quietly, why Sapo was not expelled when he so richly deserved to be. For I want as little as possible of darkness in his story. . . . I have not been able to find out why Sapo was not expelled. I shall have to leave the question open" (190). At a point well into Malone's narrative of Macmann—an avatar perhaps of Sapo, as Sapo is an avatar of Malone himself—he refers overtly to the destructive power of his own discourse: "A thousand little things to report, very strange, in view of my situation, if I interpret them correctly. But my notes have a curious tendency, as I realize at last, to annihilate all they purport to record" (259). The narrative act—the very act of writing—acknowledges in itself the impossibility of recording any substantive thing. The narratives, and indeed the extended self-analysis, thus are almost by virtue of having been recorded, epistemologically inaccurate reflections of Malone's desires: the writing moment is a moment of displacement and disfigurement of meaningful intention. If, as Gary Madison suggests in *The Hermeneutics of Postmodernity,* "the problem of 'personal identity,' of the unity and constancy of our selfhood, is nothing other than the problem of maintaining coherence and continuity in our stories" (162), the problem for Malone is the problem of the disfiguring text. Indeed, Malone's own rhetorico-critical gesture (position?) here suggests the ultimate futility of attempting to make sense of the narrative a priori in relation to the writing subject: Malone's narratives exceed his interpretive grasp; as they exceed his interpretive grasp they cease, even at the moment of their commission to the page, to act as the ordering gesture Malone desires.

The logic of the metanarrative irruption thus has a double force. First, it interpellates a self-conscious narrator into his own process of storytelling: self-consciousness thereby delimits the space of "play." Indeed, one way of reading Mallone's particular hermeneutic position here as he consistently foregrounds the fabrication of his own text is as a radical (mis)application of the hermeneutical notion of *distanciation.* I have argued in chapter 1 that Watt is as much a victim of his own inability to follow through on his hermeneutical inquiries as he is a victim of any psychological impairment. I have suggested also that Moran's subject position over the course of his narrative is informed by a particularly radical form of "hermeneutical transformation." I have suggested these readings as an ongoing attempt to figure Beckett's texts as containing within their narrative economies an unraveling of a variety of hermeneutical "problems." One way I have approached this reading is to see how the texts, which seem to have inscribed within themselves their own mode of reading, harmonize with or diverge from specific aspects of hermeneutical *theoria*. *Malone Dies,* as this chapter attempts to suggest, places the writing subject, who is also the originary hermeneuticist of the work, within the hermeneutic logic of play. Play, as Ricoeur suggests, is the mode of being of both the work of art and the hermeneutic gesture of "appropriation," a gesture, that is, which allows the interpreter to enter the "dialogue" with the text: play thus defines the interpretive act *as* interpretive. But appropriation exists in a perpetual supported balance with its opposite pole—distanciation—the pole, I suggest, thrown out of balance by Malone's inability to "be" in the game. Distanciation is a crucial component in conceiving of the integrity of text and the reader's apprehension or appropriation of it as interpretable object. Appropriation for Ricoeur means "to make one's own" what was originally "alien." Thus Ricoeur writes in "The Hermeneutical Function of Distanciation": "Distanciation is not abolished by appropriation, but is rather the counterpart of it. Thanks to distanciation by writing, appropriation no longer has any trace of affective affinity with the intention of an author. Appropriation is quite the contrary of contemporaneousness and congeniality: it is understanding at and through distance" (143). Distanciation thus allows the hermeneuticist to recognize the particular mode of being of text and the self's own mode of being in its relation to the aesthetic object: the self withdraws as the hermeneut makes the text his or her "own." "Being in play" thus involves to some extent a forgetting of one's own beingness, which is precisely the position Malone as storyteller desires to assume. Yet I think Malone's difficulties stem from an overdetermination of the hermeneutic function of distanciation: instead of allowing the appropriate "play" to occur through and within a hermeneutical distance, Malone consistently sets up distanciation as a form of pure alienation (*Verfremdung*) from text (play?): there is thus no fruitful intersubjective "dialogue" between Malone and his text; each component of the relationship maintains a separate and discrete autonomy. The failure of absorption into text moreover presupposes the impossibility of interpretation: no hermeneutic moment or dialogue can occur if the subject maintains his discrete autonomy.

Second, the metanarrative irruption functions to encode the reader's self-awareness into the text as it consolidates a kind of interpretive focus "in front" of the reader. If, as Ricoeur notes, the reader too is a playful figure in the hermeneutic encounter, a metanarrative, as it works to awaken the reader's awareness of text and textuality, works against the playful incorporation of the reader. Before looking at the consequence for the reader of the metanarrative I excerpt briefly from Ricoeur, who in "Appropriation" theorizes the reader as a "playful" figure: "It is now possible . . . to treat the reader in turn as a fictive or playful figure. For the author's subjectivity, submitted to imaginative variations, becomes a model offered by the narrator to the subjectivity of his reader. The reader as well is invited to undergo an imaginative variation of his *ego*. . . . For the work itself has constructed the reader in his role" (189). I have previously suggested that the specular reader—the reader who finds an analogue to him or herself "in" the text—undergoes a process of conferred appropriation and thus undergoes a hermeneutical-subjective transformation. Malone becomes for me the prime figure of the specular reader, as, to a lesser extent, does Watt. The position of the reader toward *Malone Dies* hinges on the blurring of subjective/ontological boundaries between reader and text; it thus seems obvious that Malone, as self-conscious narrator and hermeneut, stands as the specular reader in the text. The reader's interpretive economy is invested in "how" Malone makes sense or works to understand his present situation. But whereas the reader is incorporated gradually and has his or her hermeneutic subject position dismantled over the course of Moran's narrative in *Molloy*, in *Malone Dies* the experience is bound to a strict and abrupt dialectic of absorption into narrative and radical awareness of text and textuality. Our readerly position with regard to this text thus is continually consolidated and fractured precisely as Malone's efforts to absorb himself into texts are shattered. Thus even if, as Ricoeur suggests, a transformation of the ego occurs in the true hermeneutical encounter—and it is true that we are in a sense "transformed" as we invest a certain degree of importance in Malone's readings of his narrative and thus take up a position similar to his—the fact remains that the subjectivity of the reader is always in place as it traces through *Malone Dies:* the logic of the metanarrative denies the full "playful" erasure of the self-consciousness of the reader, just as the self-consciousness of Malone can never or will never be eradicated.

Thus we have to make some sense of the final words of the text, that moment when Malone does indeed die, as a moment of supreme irony:

> Lemuel is in charge, he raises his hatchet on which the blood will never dry, but not to hit anyone, he will not hit anyone, he will not

hit anyone any more, he will not touch anyone any more, either with it or with it or with it or with or

or with it or with his hammer or with his stick or with his fist or in thought in dream I mean never he will never

or with his pencil or with his stick or

or light light I mean

never there he will never

never anything

there

any more (288)

Malone Dies articulates itself as a parody of the topos of writing deferring death that is found, for instance, in a text like *A Thousand and One Nights*. Whereas in that text the narrative act is causally related to the deferral of death, the narratives in *Malone Dies* act not to delay death but simply to fill the void until death. Yet the narratives are linked to the thematic of death inasmuch as the "playful" desire for self-abnegation rehearses the self-forgetfulness that death itself may bring: the narratives thus may be seen as a series of little deaths: "They will be almost lifeless, like the teller" (180). The narratives themselves, however, because they do not bring about this self-forgetfulness—perhaps because for Beckett, as for Gadamer, language inscribes and "supports" Being; because Malone "is" his language—fail as the articulation of play, fail as the rehearsal for death. The irony here in these final lines is that Malone cannot inscribe the self-abnegation he desires: only a silence in the end of writing will inscribe the end of Being. The moment of play that Malone desires occurs not in the space of his texts or metatext but only as the text concludes with his death: the moment of "absolute play"—as the moment of absolute self-abnegation—is the moment of death, the uninscribable moment.

Thus I think it appropriate to echo Malone's early statement: "There I am back at my old aporetics" (181). It becomes apparent as the reader traces through Beckett's oeuvre that the aporetic split between intention and result cannot be noted simply as an "effect" (or indeed "affect") of the peculiar subject position of the perversely self-aware Beckettian narrator.

These splittings, be they narratological, temporal, or subjective, are nothing less than a major thematic of the Beckett novel. I have traced the narrative self-hermeneutic as it plays out over several texts to this point, from *Watt, Mercier and Camier, Molloy,* and now *Malone Dies:* in each case I noted the peculiar sense in which the text, either in its (con)figuration of character (*Watt*) or, more precisely, in the articulation of narrator, seems always to divide itself against itself; in all cases this division is the direct result of or is invested in the economy of *desire,* desire for narrative, desire for "directedness," order, knowledge. Malone himself expresses in what are to this point in the oeuvre the most explicit terms most clearly the desire for knowledge as knowledge of self. This desire is bound up in the "playful"—though the term belies the seriousness of the effort—gesture of the narrative as if Malone understands that the stories are in one way "about" himself. The series of narratives told by Malone thus contain in their structuration—in the very fact of their telling—an implicit desire for "coherence"; if framed as "play," the stories can be read, like the interchapter summaries of *Mercier and Camier,* as an attempt to consolidate and focus the subject of the narrative(s). But the "old aporetics" arise simultaneously with Malone's own understanding of the logic of play which demands the obfuscation of subjectivity. Subjectivity or Being is bound by language that both consolidates and defers Being or *understanding* of Being: understanding of self is mediated by that which constitutes the subject a priori. To write the end of Being thus is to engage in what Merleau-Ponty would call a "paradox of expression."[3] Subjectivity for the Beckett character thus is always painful and protracted: with the desire for the nullification of selfhood comes the realization of the impossibility of inscribing that nullification, an experience described by Blanchot in *The Gaze of Orpheus* as the "experience through which the consciousness discovers its being in its inability to lose consciousness" (33).

5

The Unnamable

> The end, the beginning, the beginning again, how can I say it, that's all words, they're all I have.
> —*The Unnamable*

> I am my world.
> —Wittgenstein, *Tractatus Logico-Philosophicus*

The Unnamable's speech is an obligatory one. It is a speech, as he describes it, conferred on him from somewhere beyond him, devoid of the speaker's own volition. It is a speech that at once articulates him as speaker and prevents the end of speech, the end of Being. It is in short—and again Beckett's speakers articulate the means of their own reading—an aporetic speech, a speech acknowledged as "speaking the speaker."[1] But because it is acknowledged as speaking the speaker, it sets itself up as distanced from the Unnamable, distanced and thus able to be perceived *as* controlling speech: the Unnamable is articulated into a state of pure self-alienation, a state that permits the recognition of discourse as being discourse. This distanciation allows the Unnamable to liberate itself from the economy of mere puppetry and to enter into a protracted self-conscious reading of its hermeneutic speech acts. The profound hermeneutic irony of *The Unnamable* is that it is this self-alienation that finally allows for a rigorous self-scrutiny, finally brings to the fore the realization that has been haunting the writers in the trilogy: Being is self-alienation; self-alienation allows for the understanding of Being-as-hermeneutics.

But the Unnamable's narrative is more than a continuation of the thematics of the aporetic subject inscribing the aporetic narrative: because the discourse is characterized as obligatory, this narrative enters into an *ethical* realm. In this chapter I attempt to give a specifically ethical reading of *The Unnamable,* to suggest how the Unnamable's "obligation" is more than logorrhoeic compulsion but is in fact an index of a profound sense of the responsibilities and power of (Being in) discourse. The responsibility of the reader of this text, I argue, is to gauge the philosophical, hermeneutic, and semiotic resonance of the notion of "obligation" as it maps out into the Unnamable's narrative, to gauge, more problematically, how the thematics of ethical obligation is manifested in a semiology—more specifically, an *aesthetic* semiology—without firm discursive or subjective boundaries. Wittgenstein proposes in the *Tractatus* that "Ethics and aesthetics are one and the same" (6.421): my analysis is an attempt to make some sense of the relation between the aesthetic act and the ethical gesture, to explore the similarity between the aesthetics of response and the ethics of response.

The question of prime importance in *The Unnamable* is that of the logic of ethics (as obligation) under the constraints of a radically fragmented subjectivity: Whence obligation for a radically decentered subject? The question of the *ethic* of speaking—and ethics here is synonymous with but not totally encompassed by the notion of obligation—is a thematic given relatively little attention in the scholarship on the Unnamable's story, even though the notion of obligation is thoroughly foregrounded and thematized in the preamble, as it is in Beckett's crucial "Three Dialogues," which I discuss below. Most critics focus on the thematics of writing and speaking in their formulations of the text. Thus Leslie Hill in *Beckett's Fiction* defines the Unnamable's speech as exhibiting an excess, "a supplement, a waste which cannot be pronounced or incorporated within words" (82). Anna Smith in "Proceeding by Aporia" maintains that the Unnamable's speech exceeds its own grasp: "Both the narrator and the narrator's language must serve as the subject and object of investigation. Perception is prior to language; language gives rise to perception. Verbal description, therefore, is never able to reveal the elusive nature of the 'I'" (21). This notion is echoed by Thomas Trezise, who notes in *Into the Breach* that the formation of the noncoincidental subject gives rise to a language unable to conceive of its own formations: "Subjectivity is the experience of a solitude. . . . Wherein, by reason of its own non-self-coincidence . . . the self as subject is *not* alone" (117). It is this noncoincidence of subject, of self and language, that leads Edouard Morot-Sir in "Grammatical Insincerity in *The Unnamable*" to note the discursive importance of the hypothesis in the Unnamable's narrative: the discourse of the hypothesis (a discourse I maintain is ineluctably related to the spirit of ethics) creates what Morot-Sir calls the "suspension" of judgment. It is in the gap between the attempt to construct a world and the reality of disfiguring discourse that the hypothesis is formed: "I propose to interpret Beckett's 'fables' as *hypotheses of Imagination,* when Imagination realizes that it cannot achieve the idealist dream of reconstructing the world and the self in the same verbal effort" (142). This curious totalizing "suspension" is an effect noted by Lawrence Miller in *Samuel Beckett: The Expressive Dilemma*. Miller writes that the narrator of *The Unnamable* "avoids any neat conclusion by adopting a method opposed to the 'spirit of system.' . . . An "aporetic approach, and the use of 'affirmations and negations invalidated as uttered' are meant to prevent any accumulation and co-ordination of assertions" (133).

It is, I think, vital to keep the "hypothetical" or "suspended" nature of the Unnamable's text counterpoised to/with his own sense of expressive obligation because it is in the space between (mere) hypothesis and the logic of obligation that the rhetorico-ethical effect of the novel is articulated. As we trace through the Unnamable's narrative, the link between nontotalizing experience and the need for acts of practical judgment in the face of this incomplete experience will become increasingly clear: although I do not wish to anticipate my argument at this point, it needs to be suggested that the acts of judgment the Unnamable will make—acts ultimately discursive or performative—are hermeneutic acts of a specifically ethical kind. The ethical act of interpretation—what I call the ethico-hermeneutic act—is ethical because made in response to and from within the lacunae of *Dasein*.

The thematic of obligation plays a large role in Beckett's own "Three Dialogues," a text often referred to as sounding some of the major themes of Beckett's oeuvre. Indeed, it is easy enough to read "Three Dialogues" into the Unnamable's own speech, to see a conjunction between "B"[eckett's] "nothing to express" and the Unnamable's "nothing to say" (314) or "What I say, what I may say, on this subject . . . has already been said" (302). It is also important to link up "B"[eckett's] "the obligation to express" with the Unnamable's oft-repeated sense of the obligation to speak. Both senses of obligation stem, I maintain, from the same space, as both articulate a corollary or concomitant obligation or ethical impulse to interpret, an ethic that resides both in the speaker-writer and in his inscribed reader.

In "Three Dialogues" the thematic of obligation is sounded a number of times:

> B-. . . Yet I speak of an art turning from it in disgust, weary of its puny exploits, weary of pretending to be able, of being able, of doing a little better the same old thing, of going a little further along a dreary road.

D-And preferring what?

B-The expression that there is nothing to express, nothing with which to express, nothing from which to express, no power to express, no desire to express, together with the obligation to express. (139)

B-The situation is that of him who is helpless, cannot act, in the event cannot paint, since he is obliged to paint. The act is of him who, helpless, unable to act, acts, in the event paints, since he is obliged to paint.

D-Why is he obliged to paint?

B-I don't know. (142)

B-I know that all that is required now, in order to bring even this horrible matter to an acceptable conclusion, is to make of this submission, this admission, this fidelity to failure, a new occasion, a new term of relation, and of the act which, unable to act, obliged to act, he makes, an expressive act, even if only of itself, of its impossibility, of its obligation. (145)

The obligation—the ethical force spurring the painter-artist-writer—is the obligation to act knowing full well the futility of action, the futility of an act (in)adequate to its own vehicle of expression. The obligation, a deeply stoic obligation in fact, is the obligation to fail. The ethic articulated by "B"(eckett) in "Three Dialogues," an ethic put into practice by the Unnamable, is therefore an ethic of *suffering*, to borrow Beckett's own term.

As Beckett suggests in *Proust*, suffering is more than a mere existential condition. It is a condition that tempers and perhaps articulates interpretation, the hermeneutical experience itself: suffering initially is a heuristic "device." It exists at the opposite pole of "Habit." As Habit disguises, perhaps disfigures the "essence" (11) and idea (of things), suffering acts to remove the veil of familiarity from experience to reveal the quiddity of that experience (Beckett's affinity with the romantics—Shelley, Coleridge—and with Brecht is obvious):[2]

> The fundamental duty of Habit, about which it describes the futile and stupefying arabesques of its supererogations, consists in a perpetual adjustment and readjustment of our organic sensibility to the conditions of its worlds. Suffering represents the omission of that duty, whether through negligence or inefficiency, and boredom its

adequate performance. The pendulum oscillates between these two terms: Suffering—that opens a window on the real and is the main condition of the artistic experience, and Boredom—with its host of top-hatted and hygienic ministers, Boredom that must be considered as the most tolerable because the most durable of human evils. (16)

Suffering—suffering of the Proustian character, the Beckettian character, the writer—thus articulates its own aesthetic, its own framing of specific experiences. The aesthetic formed within and through suffering is one of the partial, the fragmentary, the "schematic," to borrow from Ingarden. Beckett sees in Proust, and his ideas hold at least partially true for his own writing, a quasi-romantic skepticism "before causality": "Thus his [Proust's] purely logical—as opposed to his intuitive—explanations of a certain effect invariably bristle with alternatives" (61). He notes Proust's extreme subjectivism: "Consequently for the artist, the only possible hierarchy in the world of objective phenomena is represented by a table of their respective coefficients of penetration, that is to say, in terms of the subject" (64). And of course the subject for Proust and Beckett is non-self-coincidental: "The individual is a succession of individuals" (8); the subject is perhaps even defunct: "The subject has died—and perhaps many times—on the way" (3). The aesthetic production—the textual artifact—of the decentered suffering subject is constructed in this very space of incomplete knowledge, as the subject, noncoincidental to himself, is, moreover, at a remove from the object of perception: the textual product thus will be fissured, reflecting in its semiology the lacunae of the experience of Being. Beckett refers to the instability of the subject—his "mobility"—in its relation to the object and defines the (aesthetic) experience of suffering:

> Moreover, when it is a case of human intercourse, we are faced by the problem of an object whose mobility is not merely a function of the subject's, but independent and personal: two separate and immanent dynamisms related by no system of synchronisation. So that whatever the object, our thirst for possession is, by definition, insatiable. At the best, all that is realised in Time (all Time produce), whether in Art or Life, can only be possessed successively, by a series of partial annexations—and never integrally and at once. (6–7)

Beckett here outlines a problematic that should immediately remind us of the hermeneutical difficulties of, for instance, Malone, whose radical distanciation from his textual productions clearly thematizes Beckett's notion of the subject/object problematic, the difficulties produced by these "separate and immanent dynamisms."

I offer this extended introduction to the topos of obligation-as-suffering because the aesthetic that Beckett articulates in "Three Dialogues" and *Proust*—especially in its quasi-romanticism—is the aesthetic and semiology of *The Unnamable*, an aesthetic of "suspension" that articulates and delimits the semiotic (for interpretation) of both the reader and the narrator: the narrator is writing an *interpretable* object here while offering the means of its own reading, if not its own interpretation. Beckett's articulation and theory of the partial and serial possession—of what? meaning?—can, I think, be read fruitfully into an ethico-hermeneutical context that at once liberates the art object from the tyranny of the monological hermeneutic (what in my introduction I called hermetic hermeneutics) and places the reader—or writer/character *as* reader—in a responsive, dynamic space of reading. Beckett outlines an aesthetic theory that demands action on the part of the perceiver, who must consistently negotiate between aspects of the text, must negotiate a space within which to "read" the gaps and lacunae of the aesthetic object. The ethic of suffering—as an ethic of action, an ethic of interpretation—thus is conferred onto the reader. This theoretical ethic of negotiating the gaps is put into productive praxis in the Unnamable's narrative in a way that at once draws on "traditional" ethics (that we find, for instance, in Aristotle) and dismantles the very economy of the *arche* of ethical obligation. The paradoxical Beckettian strategy in *The Unnamable* is thus to use the "ghost" of a dead metaphysics to breathe life into a dead ethic.

It is not often acknowledged that the concomitant to the Unnamable's obligation to speech is his, and our, obligation to interpret. It is in fact the Unnamable's will to interpret a speech at once compelled and self-originating that places the Unnamable in, paradoxically, the clearest intellectual space of any of the narrators in the trilogy. As external signifying systems—landscape, character—fall away, the compulsion to interpret moves to the fore: as the character is reduced to mere Being (or beingness) the purest understanding of Being-as-hermeneutics arises. Thus:

> Where now? Who now? When now? Unquestioning. I, say I. Unbelieving. Questions, hypotheses, call them that. Keep going, going on, call that going, call that on. Can it be that one day, off it goes on, that one day I simply stayed in, in where, instead of going out, in the old way, out to spend day and night as far away as possible, it wasn't far.

> Perhaps that is how it began.... I seem to speak, it is not I, about me, it is not about me. These few general remarks to begin with. What am I to do, what shall I do, what should I do, in my situation, how proceed? By aporia pure and simple? Or by affirmations and negations invalidated as uttered, or sooner or later? (291)

The Unnamable's first paragraphs are the most lucid expression of the hermeneutic dilemma in Beckett, the clearest expression of the necessity to know given the limitations of the subject in epistemological crisis. The Unnamable's "And things, what is the correct attitude to adopt towards things?" (292) lays clear the interpretive problem as it rewrites the fundamental hermeneutic question: How does it stand toward me?

The Unnamable's speech thus interiorizes the opposition that defined Malone's position as aporetic: he interiorizes the opposition of speaking/being spoken only, of course, to produce more aporia, aporia that delimits itself as aporia (is it feasible then to describe self-conscious aporia as aporia?). The Unnamable's speech continues but does not complete—for how can it?—the thematic of speaking one's own dying, speaking one's own death: "One starts speaking as if it were possible to stop at will. It is better so. The search for the means to put an end to things, an end to speech, is what enables the discourse to continue" (299). Indeed, the Unnamable's speech assigns itself the dual—and perhaps exclusionary—role of articulating itself as both beginning and ending, or beginning always anticipating the end, knowing always that it inhabits the space of both polarities ("poison and antidote" [298]). But it is he, even as he is inscribed by the language of others, who assigns himself the originary role as writer, as recorder of this "Gospel" of decline: "It is I who write, who cannot raise my hand from my knee. It is I who think, just enough to write, whose head is far. I am Matthew and I am the angel, I who came before the cross, before the sinning, came into the world, came here" (301).

The Unnamable's obligation, "the compulsion I am under" (302), is to assign meaning to the logic of "Being" at the beginning, anticipating the (uninscribable?) end and thus writing the middle, the great gap of time. "But I am *here*" (301; emphasis added), says the Unnamable, and thus his preamble, his "exordia" (302), fixes the subject, defines him as subject, and clears a space for the writing of the immovable subject's story, a story that inscribes the death of the author aware of his death as he speaks his death: "And indeed I greatly fear, since my speech can only be of me and here, that I am once more again engaged in putting an end to both.... Whence a certain confusion in the exordia, long enough to situate the condemned and prepare him for execution" (302). And therefore whence a certain confusion of the writing subject, of literally, authority, who at once defines himself as an (un)willing amanuensis who must write, like Murphy's sun must rise, because he has "no alternative" (294), but who also inscribes himself as writer (Matthew) writing about himself: "So it is I who speak, all alone, since I can't do otherwise" (307). Who then, or what then, speaks here? Does the *langue* of "others" (314) become the *parole* of the Unnamable simultaneously maintaining itself as *langue*? Can *parole* exist without a speaking subject?: "It's no longer I in any case" (318). Barthes's question in *S/Z,* "Who speaks?" is the Unnamable's "Who now?" defining itself as the I without a subject, as the subject without object: "There, now there is no one here but me, no one wheels about me, no one comes towards me, no one has ever met anyone before my eyes, these creatures have never been, only I and this black void have ever been" (304).

The Unnamable thus is fully aware of the problematics of inserting the self into the "space" of *beginning* a task, is aware of the beginning as ultimately ethical because ultimately exclusive act. To begin, as Edward Said has demonstrated in *Beginnings,* is to circumscribe a space, an act of profoundly ethical resonance because it chooses to delimit "world" in the creation of "world": "A text is a statement made with signs, and those signs constitute a judgment already made that as signs they *shall be*. This judgment-statement excludes other signs, just as it includes the ones it intends. Such a way of describing a text is *ethical*" (230). The Unnamable articulates this sense of beginning as choice in his preamble:

> The thing to avoid, I don't know why, is the spirit of system. People with things, people without things, things without people, what does it matter, I flatter myself it will not take me long to scatter them, whenever I choose, to the winds. I don't see how. The best would be not to begin. But I have to begin. That is to say I have to go on. (292)[3]

> For I am obliged to assign a beginning to my residence here, if only for the sake of clarity. (295)

> It would help me, since to me I must attribute a beginning. (296)

The Unnamable's first paragraphs thus articulate themselves as an extended prolegomenon on the ethic of beginnings, the ethic—because obliged—of beginning to interpret, the ethic of attempting to inscribe the self (if the notion of the subject still obtains: "I. Who might that be?"

[336]) within a space where the logic of "understanding" may not simply be erroneous but, more problematically, irrelevant. Yet the effort to begin is in place here at the outset; the Unnamable thus articulates a desire for, if not construction of, what Said has called the "transitive" beginning intention. Such an intention "foresees a continuity flowing from it" (76); it is what Benveniste in his essay "Language and Human Experience" calls the "axial moment which provides the zero point of the computation" (5): it is, in philosophical terms, the articulation of a desire for the *arche*, or what Derrida in *Writing and Difference* somewhat meanspiritedly calls "an ethic of nostalgia for origins" (292).

Articulating or inscribing a beginning is thus an act of profound epistemologico-hermeneutic consequences: it is the logic of beginning as ground (*arche*) that presupposes the movement toward end (*telos*). But the Unnamable's narrative calls on a kind of thinking about the logic of beginning that he will acknowledge to be defunct. And yet what prevents the narrative from simply articulating itself as protracted aporia is this profound sense of obligation, a sense that seems at once to call on what Derrida would term "metaphysical" categories and casts into doubt the very ground (*arche*) of that thinking. As in *Mercier and Camier, Molloy,* and *Malone Dies,* we again see here a double movement in the narrative: there is at once the desire to dismantle the very (ethical) system that seems to prop up the facticity of the narrative. Moreover, the Unnamable's obligation—to express, to interpret—is a constitutive "metaphysical" category that prevents the radical and absolute dismantling of the "logic" of ethics as it prevents the absolute dismantling of the subject: the concomitant obligation to interpret, I suggest, carries with it an implicit ethical component that will recompose the economy of ethics even as the Unnamable tries to dismantle it. The Unnamable's narrative does not simply dismantle the "logic" of ethics but acknowledges the force of the ethical obligation by questioning its efficacy in a purely discursive context.

Thus it is the resonance of the Unnamable's "must" that configures his speech—as action, as interpretation—as ethical in the sense described, for instance, by J. Hillis Miller in *The Ethics of Reading*. Miller speaks about the ethics of reading, which for me encompasses also the ethics of speech in the Unnamable's discourse: speech, writing, reading, and interpretation are conflated and interpenetrating categories in Beckett's oeuvre. Miller writes: "The ethical moment in the act of reading, then, if there is one, faces in two directions. On the one hand it is a response to something, responsible to it, responsive to it, respectful of it. In any ethical moment there is an imperative, some 'I must' or *Ich Kann nicht anders*. I *must* do this. I cannot do otherwise. . . . On the other hand, the ethical moment in reading leads to an act" (4). For the Unnamable the moment of speech/writing/reading/interpretation does not have the necessary (according to Miller) concomitant of action: it *is* action. It is always an action. The concomitant act here is, of course, the actual reader's reading of the Unnamable's *multisemiotic*. But the problem here for the reader is to locate within the fractured sensibility or subjectivity of the narrator the locus of the ethic: an ethic to be an ethic must be identifiable as such, must presuppose an origin (*arche*) of the obligatory force. The Unnamable's ethic of "must" comes from himself, comes from "elsewhere": it is both exterior and interior to himself: "This voice that speaks, knowing that it lies . . . it is not mine, I can't stop it, I can't prevent it, from tearing me, racking me, assailing me. It is not mine, I have none, I have no voice and must speak, that is all I know, its round that I must revolve, of that I must speak, with this voice that is not mine, but can only be mine, since there is no one but me" (307). Indeed, it is from within this problematic configuration of speaking/spoken "voices" (to call the novel "dialogical" is to beg the question of originary sources of the voice) that the Unnamable recognizes the difficulty of even articulating his obligation *as* obligation:

> Strange notion in any case, and eminently open to suspicion, that of a task to be performed, before one can be at rest. Strange task, which consists in speaking of oneself. Strange hope, turned towards silence and peace. Possessed of nothing but my voice, the voice, it may seem natural, once the idea of obligation has been swallowed, that I should interpret it as an obligation to say something. But is it possible? (311)

The Unnamable's difficulty here is, in short, as much a problem of ethics as it is one of speaking/being spoken/being unable to speak/ceasing speaking/ceasing being spoken. It is a problem of locating the impelling force of the obligation: does it reside within the narrator or without?

The Unnamable will suppose "that it is in fact required of me that I say something, something that is not found in all I have said up to now. That seems a reasonable assumption. But thence to infer that the something required is something about me strikes me as unwarranted" (311). And thus the difficulty of locating the source, the *arche* of the obligatory force is subsumed by the narrator under the larger question of language: the question becomes one of locating or defining the nature of ethical action in the Unnamable's universe of pure language. I posited in my introduction that the ethical component to interpretation is formed by the constant hermeneutical application of *action* in the space between text and reader. The Beckett text compels its reader continually to negotiate and adjust his or her ethico-interpretive bearing in negotiating the Beckettian aporia: to read Beckett is to engage actively in purposeful interpretive action. This action is impelled by the facticity of the reader/text relationship—the very reality of the hermeneutic encounter compels the hermeneutic dialogue or negotiation. The fundamental premise of ethics is that one inserts oneself into a situation where obligation or action arises *actually:* that is, there is some course of action to be decided on.

The Beckett character is often inscribed within the configuration of the ethical or what I have been calling the *phronetic* moment (*phronesis:* practical or prudent judgment/action). The common expression of this ethic is the desire to know how to act in and interpret a specific situation: this moment is one I wish to figure as the ethico-hermeneutical moment. I want to pause here and outline the importance of *phronesis* as it pertains to *The Unnamable* and specifically its pertinence to a Gadamerian hermeneutics. Gadamer borrows the concept from Aristotle's *Ethics* and draws parallels between ethical action and hermeneutic action using the concept of *phronesis* as a yoke. In Part II of *Truth and Method* Gadamer draws explicitly on the ethical resonance of hermeneutics specifically by reference to the *Ethics*. Aristotle is important to Gadamer's project in that Aristotle figures ethics as a practical response to the task at hand: "But what interests us here is precisely that he [Aristotle] is concerned with reason and with knowledge, not detached from a being that is becoming, but determined by it and determinative of it" (*Truth and Method* 312). Moreover, the ethical action is a practical judgment based explicitly on the exigencies of the immediate context, a context in which full knowledge may not obtain; Aristotle makes the point that ethical action, since it must conform to the task at hand that never fully reveals itself, cannot account for the totality of human experience: ethical action situates itself as a practical partial response to a totality which is perhaps beyond immediate comprehension: "For the scientific truth is demonstrable, whereas art and prudence (*phronesis*) are only concerned with the variable" (*Ethics* 211). Gadamer writes: "In contrast to the theory of the good based on Plato's doctrine of ideas, Aristotle emphasizes that it is impossible for ethics to achieve the extreme exactitude of mathematics. Indeed, to demand this kind of exactitude would be inappropriate. What needs to be done is simply to make an outline and by means of this sketch give some help to moral consciousness" (313). As ethical knowledge is not "pure" knowledge, so too for Gadamer hermeneutical knowledge is constructed in a balance of practical judgment and incomplete experience: "This is the point at which we can relate Aristotle's analysis of moral knowledge to the hermeneutical problem of the modern human sciences. Admittedly, hermeneutical consciousness is involved neither with technical nor moral knowledge, but these two types of knowledge still include *the same task of application* that we have recognized as the central problem of hermeneutics" (315). Gary Madison picks up this line of argument in *The Hermeneutics of Postmodernity*:

> Moreover, unlike theoretical reason, whose purpose is to lead one to an insight into what simply is and which, in principle, exists as what it is independently of the knowing subject, practical reason is concerned with all those situations where one must make a choice, produce something, or decide on a course of action, the outcome of which is contingent in that it depends, precisely, on the subject oneself. This is another reason why practical reason should be taken as the model for interpretation, for interpretation too is always a creative business. (34)

The interpretive moment in Beckett is ethical inasmuch as it is often an obligatory moment of compelled action in the face of incomplete or undisclosed knowledge. It is also a moment that may, or may not, have consequences beyond the immediate sphere of the sole actor. The trilogy, however, pares down the *act-consequence* element of ethics by inscribing its characters within increasingly solipsistic "spaces." The large ethical questions I think the trilogy in toto raises are: Does the ethical moment exist if the actant is isolated purely? What kind of practical judgment is involved in a purely discursive moment? *Can the ethical moment be a moment of pure discourse?* The question here shares something with Wittgenstein's observation in the *Tractatus* of "world" existing as the very limits of language: "*The limits of my language* mean the limits of my world" (5.6); yet for Wittgenstein, as for, I suggest, the Unnamable, there is some "truth" in solipsism as the "intending" proposition (or consciousness) is in place (5.62). For Wittgenstein, as for the Unnamable, world is a function of the subject, not vice versa: "The subject does not belong to the world: rather, it is a limit of the world" (5.632). The responsibility of the reader of *The Unnamable* is to make sense of the Unnamable's semiology in terms of the ethic he creates when he says, to borrow again from the *Tractatus,* "I am my world" (5.63).

The Unnamable articulates himself in a space that perhaps even moves beyond pure solipsism in that there seems even no "I" to speak of: "I. Who might that be?" (336). The narrator, rather, configures himself as neither one thing nor another; he is a liminal, or more precisely, a hymenal figure: "I'm neither one side nor the other, I'm in the middle, I'm the partition, I've two surfaces and no thickness, perhaps that's what I feel, myself vibrating, I'm the tympanum, on the one hand the mind, on the other the world, I don't belong to either" (383). Indeed, it might be more accurate to posit the Unnamable, as he himself will do, as existing in a "world" of pure discourse:

> I'm in words, made of words, others' words, what others, the place too, the air, the walls, the floor, the ceiling, all words, the whole world is here with me, I'm the air, the walls, the walled-in one, everything yields, opens, ebbs, flows, like flakes, I'm all these flakes, meeting, mingling, falling asunder, wherever I go I find me . . . a particle of me, retrieved, lost, gone astray, I'm all these words, all these strangers, this dust of words, with no ground for their settling. (386)[4]

Thus the question: Whence obligation in this "wurdy-gurdy" (399), this world of pure discourse without ground, without *arche*? Despite the obvious totalizing discursivity of the Unnamable's universe—a discursivity that as it is defined here seems to preclude full apprehension of *Dasein*— the obligation to seek, to find an *arche* and *telos* is there: "I'm always seeking something, it's tiring in the end, and it's only my beginning" (387). But despite momentary hallucinations of a unitary subject—"there is I, yes, I feel it, I confess, I give in, there is I, it's essential, it's preferable" (388)—hypotheses of the obliged "I" give way to hypotheses of the decentered subject: "It has not yet been our good fortune to establish with any degree of accuracy what I am, where I am, whether I am words among words, or silence in the midst of silence, to recall only two of the hypotheses launched in this connexion" (388). And thus the suffering of pure discourse—as the suffering of pure Being—leads the narrator to propose, as a solution to the gaps of experience/knowledge, as a *phronetic* act of judgment and *creation*, the efficacy of "resolutions" (389):

> More resolutions, while we're at it, that's right, resolutely, more resolutions. *Make* abundant use of the principle of parsimony, as if it were familiar to me, it is not too late. *Assume* notably henceforward that the thing said and the thing heard have a common source, resisting for this purpose the temptation to call in question the possibility of assuming anything whatever. *Situate* this source in me,

without specifying where exactly, no finicking, anything is preferable to the consciousness of third parties and, more generally speaking, of an outer world. *Carry* if necessary this process of compression to the point of abandoning all other postulates than that of a deaf half-wit, hearing nothing of what he says and understanding even less. *Evoke* at painful junctions, when discouragement threatens to raise its head, the image of a vast cretinous mouth, red, blubber and slobbering, in solitary confinement, extruding indefatigably, with a noise of wet kisses and washing in a tub, the words that obstruct it. *Set aside* once and for all, at the same time as the analogy with orthodox damnation, all idea of beginning and end. *Overcome*, that goes without saying, the fatal leaning towards expressiveness. *Equate* me, without pity or scruple, with him who exists, somehow, no matter how, no finicking, with him whose story this story had the brief ambition to be. Better, *ascribe* to me a body. Better still, *arrogate* me a mind. *Speak* of a world of my own, sometimes referred to as the inner, without choking. *Doubt* no more. *Seek* no more. *Take* advantage of the brand-new soul and substantiality to abandon, with the only possible abandon, deep down within. And finally, these and other decisions having been taken, *carry on* cheerfully as before. (389–90; emphasis added)

This series of imperatives—compelling whom? the narrator? the reader?—act as performatives, discursively calling into Being that state required through and within which to act in accordance with the narrator's own self-described ethic of obligation. They construct a stability of discourse, an *arche* of discourse ("the thing said and the thing heard have a common source"); they construct discursively a stability of body and mind; they in fact command discursively the cessation of the aporia that would seem to preclude the ability to act ethically. The Unnamable's brutally ironic "Doubt no more" contains the maximum compression of the *phronetic* act: he has made in this statement an imaginative performative resolution toward a stability of Being, or, as Wittgenstein would have it, the propositions the Unnamable offers create an imagined "model of reality."

Yet these performatives exist only discursively, and thus the question: Whence obligation in a world of pure discourse? can it seems be answered for the Unnamable only negatively: there is no obligation. This answer, however, again begs the question of the narrator's own finely attuned sense of the impetus and obligation to speak, to go on speaking about an obligation without *arche*, without authority, without beginning or end: "Set aside once and for all . . . all idea of beginning and end." But ethics, as Aristotle astutely noticed, is all about delimiting *arche* and *telos*: "For the originative cause [*arche*] of an action is the purpose [*telos*] for which it is done" (*Ethics* 210). The narrator's setting aside of the logic of beginning and end is more than the deconstruction of the origin, more than an inscription of an absence at the center of structure: it is a paradoxical acknowledgment of an end to the delimiting prescriptions of *arche* and *telos* while maintaining the need for obligatory force, regardless of how the reading or interpreting subject—or indeed how the interpretable situation itself—is figured or (re)inscribed by that obligating force. *The Unnamable*, which thus at once decomposes the subject into various simulacra (Worm, Mahood) and various "pronouns" (404)—and thereby threatens the basis of ethical action by splitting the ethical "actant"— curiously recomposes "it" via the logic and economy of aporetic obligation, aporetic because having no source, being neither internal nor external to the narrator, it being neither one thing nor the other, but still an *obligation*. It needs to be emphasized that regardless of the effort to rid itself of the logic of beginning and ending, of the logic of the subject, the philosophical basis (*arche*) of the narrator's ethic of suffering (as obligation) will always reinscribe that which it attempts to "outlive." The very fact of a sense of obligation—to continue, to express, to suffer—is the inscription of an ethic, and the inscription of an ethic will always threaten to reinscribe the subject even as the subject places himself under erasure. Edward Said, to return to his *Beginnings*, calls this aporetic moment the "intransitive beginning":

> It is very much a creature of the mind, very much a bristling paradox, yet also very much a figure of thought that draws special attention to itself. Its existence cannot be doubted, yet its pertinence is wholly to itself. Because it cannot truly be known, because it belongs more to silence than it does to language, because it is what has always been left behind, and because it challenges continuities that go cheerfully forward with *their* beginnings obediently affixed—it is therefore something of a necessary fiction. (77)

The narrator's will-to-narrate (as a will-to-create)—a will shared in part by Malone—thus has the characteristics both of willed *phronetic* act, that is, a discourse creating a possible ethical "world," and of the fragmentive, the partial: it creates a discourse that Gadamer in *Hegel's Dialectic* calls "speculative," discourse that "points to an entirety of truth, without being that entirety or stating it" (96), a discourse that must have something of the "silent" about it. We may in fact characterize the entire narrative of the Unnamable as constructed on the dialectic of the *phronetic* and the "speculative": it is in the space between these two poles that the (moribund) ethical energy of the text obtains because the "speculative," that is, incomplete, nature of this discourse continually demands a response, continually demands an active hermeneutic. Thus the Unnamable: "I go on as best I can, if it begins to mean something I can't help it" (400); and thus the responsibilities of the storytelling act that composes a unity of discourse and subjectivity even as it must dismantle that unity:

> his story the story to be told, but he has no story, he hasn't been in story, it's not certain, he's in his own story, unimaginable, unspeakable, that doesn't matter, *the attempt must be made,* in the old stories incomprehensibly mine, to find his, it must be there somewhere, it must have been mine, before being his, I'll recognize it, in the end I'll recognize it, the story of the silence that he never left, that I should never have left, that I may never find again, that I may find again, then it will be he, it will be I, it will be the place, the silence, *the end, the beginning, the beginning again, how can I say it, that's all words, they're all I have.* (413; emphasis added)

And thus we have circled back to the question of ethics in a purely discursive context: ethics, as an orienting response to the vagaries and variabilities of Being, is a fact or, perhaps more radically, a result of being-in-the-world, is the fact of being-in-language. The dynamic response to the lacunae of *Dasein*—and I have read the above excerpted passages as provisional *phronetic* responses—is the formulation of hermeneutic *phronesis:* the ethic of hermeneutics is an ethic as it orients itself from and toward an *interpretable* discursive situation, that is, a situation itself always already polysemous. The logic of this formulation is that any situation is potentially interpretable and hence demanding of an ethical response: the very fact of being-in-the-world (the hermeneutics of *Dasein*) is *necessarily* ethical.

My reading of *The Unnamable* is intended to suggest that the split between the subject and his discourse, instead of negating the possibility or even the premise of ethico-hermeneutic action, itself is productive of it. In fact, the split is what allows me to read the semiology of the text *as* ethical: the split creates the polysemous nature of the discourse, that is, creates the very need for interpretation. It inscribes a polyvalent subject confronted with a "world" of pure and hence interpretable discourse. If the ethical situation is in the widest sense "dialogical" in that there must be two components to the ethical and hermeneutical exchange (a thing to oblige, a thing to be obliged; a thing to be interpreted, a thing to interpret), the Unnamable has (unwittingly?) created an ethical situation it perhaps cannot even comprehend *as* ethical in its own self-described solipsism. And thus the narrator's "I can't go on, I'll go on" (414) is the inscription—and perhaps it can only be an inscription—of a self-imposed ethical obligation that acknowledges itself as a purely discursive act: the only (ethical) response to the "silence" is discourse—"I'll go on, you must say words, as long as there are any" (414)—because the silence is that which negates the possibility of reaching the (always already dismantled) end: "in the silence you don't know" (414).

The "end" of this discourse of silence is a semiotic that itself demands or "obliges" the reader: it is a semiotic (of "suffering") that is itself *ethical* as it demands an ethical, that is, factical, *phronetic* response from the reader, a response geared toward the present instance of discourse (this entire chapter thus stands as one such response). Such a response, moreover, is not one, I suggest, guided by the theological hermeneutic and promise of the "revelatory" text; rather, the ethical response is more radically one that demands a construction of a paradigm of reading, a "way" or "method" that articulates itself in the balance between the reader's "prejudice" (*Vorgriff*) and affect of the text. It is a method of reading that is itself speculative as it is "fully unfinished"; it is what Gadamer calls *Bildung:* a continual process that confirms the exigencies of text as it conforms to that text's own first premises. This is not to say that the reader is "bound" to the text or its reading: the reading takes place "in between" text and reader (as in play), in the interstices of hermeneutical dialogue. It should be apparent that this situation is as much a description of *The Unnamable*'s hermeneutic as it is one of the reader's: *The Unnamable* in a peculiar way thus confirms, as it articulates, the hermeneutic circle, which is simply another way of saying that Beckett's texts always already inscribe their readers even as they reinscribe the basic hermeneutical question: How does it stand toward me? And thus the response to the overarching question posed by *The Unnamable*—whence ethics in a purely discursive context?—can be answered: in the reader.

6

How It Is

> my life last state last version ill-said ill-heard
> ill-recaptured ill-murmured in the mud
> brief movements of the lower face losses everywhere
> —*How It Is*

How It Is ties together all the hermeneutic threads that make up the previous novels. It thematizes the questions of the semiotics of repetition, the problematics of temporality, and the integrity of the narrator as written/writing subject, questions that inform to a greater or lesser degree all of *Watt, Mercier and Camier, Molloy, Malone Dies*, and *The Unnamable*. It diverges from the previous texts in the corpus in its structural arrangement, in its conflating of the teleological impulse—"how it was I quote before Pim with Pim after Pim how it is three parts I say it as I hear it" (7)—with the fracturing effect of parataxis: "instead of ending abandoned I end as tormentor/ the essential would seem to be lacking/ this solitude when the voice recounts it sole means of living it" (129). *How It Is* is a text that rewrites the notion of narrative even as it presents a self-consciously "linear" narrative in a productively, and paradoxically, paratactical form. Thus a hermeneutic reading of a text such as *How It Is* will be as much a hermeneutic of form—*configuration*—as it is a hermeneutic of the function of narrative in what may be called a nondiscursive or non-narrative semiological context.[1]

In this pivotal text Beckett moves from thematizing a particular hermeneutic problem to a more generalized thematization of a hermeneutic of *being*: the fundamental question this text explores is that of the (hermeneutic) subject articulated in a general economy of suffering. But because *How It Is* (re)presents itself as an extended paratactical quotation: "how it was I quote" (7), it immediately configures and articulates itself "in" the discursive space of repetition, and thus the entire problematic of the representation of repetition instantiates the difficulty of "locating" the present moment of Being and, more precisely, the present moment of *suffering* in the narrator's story. What is at stake in this text of "midget grammar" (76) is the efficacy of representation, the representation of the facticity of suffering in the discursive space of repetition, the space, to borrow from Heidegger's *Being and Time,* of "having-been" (388). The crucial question *How It Is* presents to us is a narratological, thus ultimately a hermeneutical one: *when* is suffering? I will read *How It Is* through a matrix of converging hermeneutic lenses all of which touch on or use as a point of departure this thematic of the (a)temporality of suffering. In the first section I discuss the semiotics of memory and subjectivity; in the second, using some aspects of Deleuze's writings on the subject, the semiotics of desire and the Other; and in the third, using Blanchot (using Heidegger), the semiotics of death and writing. All three sections in turn detail the complex relation between memory, desire, death, and the constitution of the narrating subject from whom the logic of suffering gathers its authority: "only one voice here yes mine yes" (144–45).

The question—when is suffering?—is problematized at the outset of *How It Is* by the configuration of the speaking/narrating/narrated voice:

> past moments old dreams back again as fresh like those that pass or things things always and memories I say them as I hear them murmur them in the mud in me that were without when the panting stops scraps of an ancient voice in me not mine (7)

The text resurrects again the thematics of voice explored in *The Unnamable,* the problematic of speaking yet being simultaneously spoken. Indeed, fixing the precise "ontology" of the speaker is a concern of critics. Eric P. Levy in *Beckett and the Voice of Species,* for instance, figures the narrator unproblematically as the "Bom" named in the text (84), a gesture that does little to acknowledge the text's thematization of the very problem of the speaking "I." In *Wandering and Home: Beckett's Metaphysical Narrative,* Eyal Amiran chooses rather to see the question of the subject as one of deciphering a problematic of the Neoplatonic One and the many: by figuring the question in specifically metaphysical terms, Amiran, though acknowledging the polyvocality of the subject, finally inscribes the text within a philosophical paradigm the "metaphysics" of which the text—and indeed oeuvre—may in fact resist or nullify. In *Beckett's Fiction: In Different Words,* Leslie Hill chooses to let the narrator remain anonymous or to be effaced entirely in a manner that simply ignores the difficulty of locating the subject in the text (140).

Part of my argument in what follows is predicated on the observation that the subject in this text articulates himself in a space "ontically" separate from the semiotic space of memory. The critical readings of *How It Is* are problematic because they tend to reify the subject in a textual context that explicitly resists that reification: to perceive a subject in this text is to perceive a problematic of the subject without memory and thus without that which constitutes the subject as subject, as I shall argue below. The question here in *How It Is* thus is not one of the identity of the speaker but of the temporality of the speaker because temporality always determines the "being" and thus the subjectivity of the suffering subject, as Gadamer notes in *Truth and Method*. Commenting on Heidegger's configuration of being *in* time Gadamer writes: "What being is was to be determined from within the horizon of time. Thus the structure of temporality appeared as ontologically definitive of subjectivity. . . . Heidegger's thesis was that being itself is time" (*Truth and Method* 257). Gadamer goes on to offer a comment on the ontology of the subject that seems to me a superb definition of the (non?) ontology of the speaker in *How It Is* and, more precisely, the epistemological position of the speaker who is, in Gadamer's terms, both "knower" and "known": "Neither the knower nor the known is 'present-at-hand' in an 'ontic' way, but in a 'historical' one—that is, they both have the mode of being of historicity" (*Truth and Method* 261).[2]

The speaker of *How It Is* is acutely aware of himself as a historically located subject, crawling through a phenomenal world—"in the mud" (7)—seemingly untouched by the movements of temporality but at the same time aware of "vast tracts of time" (7). Part of the peculiarity of the speaker—and part of his anxiety as historically located consciousness—is his sense of history continually offset by his overwhelming sense of the intractable present, the unchanging order of the now; this unchanging now, however, is articulated within the logic of repetition and thus confers a specific aporetic onto the present: "here then part one how it was before Pim we follow I quote the natural order more or less my life last state last version what remains bits and scraps I hear it my life natural order more or less I learn it I quote a given moment long past vast stretch of time on from there that moment and following not all a selection natural order vast tracts of time" (7). The present moment that is articulated by its place at the "end" of the vast tract of time, this "last version" that we know is only a last version of an endlessly repeating version, is a moment articulated "vertically" by its awareness of the past "above." In part one of *How It Is* the speaker articulates a fairly clear relation between the linear present now (I say "linear" as a metaphor for the speaker's sense of *telos* or continuity "in" the vast tracts of time) and the vertically oriented memory of the life "above" in the light. These memories are arranged in or intrude on the present now as moments of absolute revelation or, to borrow again from Heidegger, *aletheia*. In fact, these memories are more than memories: they are constructed images that "reveal" the space between the now and the then, or the point of the intersection of the two temporalities. I list a series of images:

> life in the light first image some creature or other I watched him after my fashion from afar through my spy-glass sidelong in mirrors through windows at night first image (9)

> another image so soon again a woman looks up looks at me the images come at the beginning part one they will cease I say it as I hear it murmur it in the mud the images part one how it was before Pim I see them in the mud a light goes on they will cease a woman I see her in the mud

> she sits aloof ten yards fifteen yards she looks up looks at me says at last to herself all is well he is working (10)

> the huge head hatted with birds and flowers is bowed down over my curls the eyes burn with severe love I offer her mine pale upcast to the sky whence cometh our help and which I know perhaps even then with time shall pass away (15)

> another image yet another a boy sitting on a bed in the dark or a small old man I can't see with his head be it young or be it old his head in his hands I appropriate that heart (18)

> another image above in the light you come to in hospital in the dark (22)

> I look to me about sixteen and to crown all glorious weather egg-blue sky and scamper of little clouds I have my back turned to me and the girl too whom I hold who holds me by the hand the arse I have (29)

By figuring the subject in the interstices of this vertical-horizontal parataxis (I do not think of the relation as a dialectical one) the text thus metaphorizes, or doubles the metaphorization of, temporality and being *spatially* in a manner that estranges—and perhaps parodies—the epistemology and metaphorization of time, space, and being. The speaker of *How It Is* finds himself (or creates himself, or is created) in the curious semiological position of "being" at the "point" intersecting temporal-"horizontal" ("vast tracts of time") and temporal-"vertical" lines: "life life the other above in the light said to have been mine on and off no going back up there no question no one asking that of me never there a few images on and off in the mud earth sky a few creatures in the light some still standing" (8). The peculiar position of this speaker is thus to have lived a life and to be living a life: the life above in the "light" is one so distant, so remote, as to be a completely different level or order of Being. And the life below *now* in the mud is one of an eternal present continually aware of its position on a repeated and repeating continuum. The contradiction or aporia in this temporal position defines the speaker as living in a repeated present moment continually (un)aware of the repeatable past, as Ursula K. Hiese notes in "*Erzahlzeit* and Postmodern Narrative": the "logic" of repetition here configures a contradiction in and at the level of the textual representation of temporality (262). The textual *now* simultaneously configures itself as quoted *then*. Hiese notes that the reader must keep both temporalities in view while proceeding through the text and "must understand it [the text] as a flickering, an alternation of both. . . . Both readings logically exclude each other and yet are simultaneously present" (262). Defining the present moment of suffering thus becomes a problem of divining the presentness of the past or the pastness of the present.

As they intersect with the present moment—and narrative—of the now, the images seem to offer an alternative narrative; they seem to articulate an alternative plane of being that contrasts the "history" of a past life with the present one in the mud. This doubling, however, produces an effect that needs to be understood as more than merely a conflation of past and present temporalities into one discursive semiotic zone. To see an alternative narrative in these images is to go some ways toward "naturalizing" the present moment of the narrating "I": to place these images hermeneutically in "dialogue" with the present moment is to place the present moment—itself perhaps unlocatable—within an arbitrary frame of understanding, as if, as has been suggested, this "now" is the dim "afterlife" to the life constructed or suggested in the images.[3] To embrace such a reading produces some difficulties. First, it tends to elide the problematic of temporality into a clear binary of past and present, a binary which the logic of repetition consistently threatens to deconstruct. Second, these images instantiate a fairly clear and readable conventional "life" (in fact, those critics given to biographical readings will find a mine of detail from Beckett's own life in these images), a conventional life that stands in absolute—one might say *generic*—antithesis to the absurd present moment, a moment so improbable as to articulate itself on the boundary line of allegory. The arrangement of these images—images of boyhood, motherhood, love, death—alongside the present now produces a bizarre and uncanny generic struggle between memory and allegory which itself problematizes the notion of clear relations between the image and the speaker, between the past and the present. The point to foreground here is again how the text—formally—problematizes the notions of relation and representation, how even the discursive articulation of memory itself is productive of a distance in the knowing re-membering subject: memory as memory "exists" in another semiotic plane, indeed perhaps in a different *semiosis* altogether. If the subject—reading, writing, knowing—is the product of memory, is, in a sense, a function of memory, we have here at least a split subject or, perhaps even more radically, an unknowable because unknowing subject.

I have posited this text as articulating the suffering subject in the zone or space of "repetition." The narrator's discourse is generative—"a word from me and I am *again*" (26; emphasis added)—but productive of an unknowing/unknowable subject because beyond, or is it below?, memory: he inhabits, in his own perfect words, "an under-earth where I am inconceivable" (37). The text's entire problematic can, I think, be filtered through this subjective matrix: to exist beyond or below memory is to exist in a semiosis without a subject, as subjectivity—the sense of one's own being or selfhood—is itself the product of memory, itself in turn functioning semiotically within *time*. And thus we have circled back to the primary question: *when is suffering*? If it is time that articulates the subject, or articulates the grounds for understanding the subject, we have to recognize how *How It Is,* as it frames itself in repetition, problematizes this understanding of subjectivity and Being. The narrator presents his text as extended quotation and thus immediately figures it as simulacrum:[4] "my life last state last version ill-said ill-heard ill-recaptured ill-murmured in the mud" (7). But as simulacrum—as repeated "version"— it resists temporality. The original version of events is placed in infinite regress even as the "present" moment is enveloped by the logic of the quotation: "I quote the natural order more or less my life . . . I quote a given moment long past vast stretch of time" (7). Thus to locate a "given moment" (of suffering) is only to locate its simulacrum, its quotation within a structure *itself* functioning from the "unthinkable first to the no less unthinkable last" (140) as extended "inconceivable" repetition.

The subject's status as simulacrum thus inaugurates a seemingly irresolvable ontological problem in *How It Is:* to apprehend the subject as simulacrum is, as Jean Baudrillard would put it, to displace the real, the real from and to which suffering as suffering must orient itself. In *Simulations,* Baudrillard writes of the simulacrum: "It is rather a question of substituting signs of the real for the real itself, that is, an operation to deter every real process by its operational double" (4). The simulacrum as "image" is always a "murderer of the real" (10) as it reduces the real by simulation into signs of the real, a "radical negation of the sign as value" (11). At this point in my analysis of *How It Is* the subject has been articulated as simulacrum, as repeated version of itself and thus as an instantiation of an unlocatable moment of suffering. But this is perhaps only one-half of the story in *How It Is* because part two explicitly dramatizes the subject as a desiring subject, a subject in relation to an Other that acts as inscribable/torturable body.[5] I argue that the narrator here cannot be left simply as aporetic subject-as-simulacrum: it is the fact of *desire* that threatens to recompose the narrating subject, to make him "conceivable" again. Indeed, the text's instantiation of desire can be read as a reconfiguration of what Baudrillard would call the (hallucinatory) power of representation. If simulation, or the order of simulacra, inaugurates a negation of the sign as value, representation initiates a metaphysics of presence, an equivalence of the sign and the real. I argue in what follows that the body of the (torturable) Other functions as the sign of the real in *How It Is,* functions as the means by which to recognize the subject in a metaphysics of presence. Ultimately, I suggest that the narrator of *How It Is* articulates himself in the aporetic interstices between representation and simulation, always seeing himself shimmering between the real and its murderous image.

As he places the subject in this paratactical "abyss" of self-consciously produced texuality, Beckett thematizes the process of desire, desire for the Other as articulable text and as inscribable body through which to (self-)create the writing subject; the narrator attempts to "conceive" the writing subject through the written body of the Other.[6] I borrow from Gilles Deleuze here, who articulates a theory of desire in his *Dialogues*. Desire for Deleuze in not articulated in a "lack":

Do you realize how simple a desire is? Sleeping is a desire. Walking is a desire. Listening to music, or making music, or writing, are desires. . . . Old age also is a desire. Even death. Desire never needs interpreting, it is that which experiments . . . it is objected that by releasing desire from lack and law, the only thing we have left to refer to is a state of nature, a desire that would be natural and spontaneous reality. We say quite the opposite: *desire only exists when assembled or machined.* You cannot grasp or conceive of a desire outside a determinate assemblage. (136)

It is Deleuze's notion of the assembled or machined nature of desire that I find fruitful for a reading of *How It Is,* a text transparently "machined"— as self-conscious articulation of process: "similarly number 814326 may know by repute number 814345 number 814344 having spoken of him to number 814343" (120). Moreover, the text, in its obsessive concern with process over ground (through the mud) seems the perfect emblem of Deleuze and Guattari's notion, articulated in *A Thousand Plateaus: Capitalism and Schizophrenia,* of the "territorial assemblage" (503).[7] Thus I think we can account for the narrative as process and configuration in territory, as an articulating expression of desire purely. It is the narrator who is "signifying again I'm subject to these whims" (88); it is his "composition" (52) that orders things; it is he who has the power to "efface myself behind my creature" (52). Most purely—and it *is* "sadism pure and simple" (63)—it is the narrator who uses Pim's body as a space for his "literature," a space to write the moment toward death (I will return to Blanchot below): "with the nail then of the right index I carve and when it breaks or falls until it grows again with another on Pim's back intact at the outset from left to right and top to bottom as in our civilisation I carve my Roman capitals" (70). This moment of inscription on the body, as in Kafka's "The Penal Colony," establishes writing as profoundly an articulation of power; it is the writing that deictically "fixes" this particular victim in the muddy now of this atemporality, this memoryless space:

> YOUR LIFE HERE long pause YOUR LIFE HERE good and deep long pause this dead soul what appal I can imagine YOUR LIFE unfinished for murmur light of day light of night little scene HERE to the quick and someone kneeling or huddled in a corner in the gloom start of little scene in the gloom HERE HERE to the bone the nail breaks quick another in the furrows HERE HERE howls thump the whole face in the mud mouth nose no more breath and howls (96)

In Kafka, however, there is a discernible difference in "ontology" between the punisher and the punished. In *How It Is* the punisher in his turn will move into the position of punished, but, more important, his position as memoryless subject is precisely that of his victim. He speaks as much about himself as his victim here: "they are not memories no he has no memories no nothing to prove he was ever above no in the places he sees no but he may have been yes skulking somewhere yes hugging the walls yes by night yes he can't affirm anything no deny anything no so one can't speak of memories no but at the same time one can speak of them yes" (97). There is in this passage a curious and paradoxical conflation of desires: the desire to fix the victim in memoryless space and the desire, it seems, to access through the aporia of the now the impossible possibility of memory, of being. We can, I think, understand this moment as what Deleuze in the *Logic of Sense* describes as a "paradox of becoming":

> Becoming unlimited comes to the ideational and incorporeal event, with all of its characteristic reversals between future and past, active and passive, cause and effect, more or less, too much and not enough, already and not yet. The infinitely divisible event is always *both at once*. It is eternally that which has just happened and that which is about to happen, but never that which is happening (to cut too deeply and not enough). The event, being itself impassive, allows the active and the passive to be interchanged more easily, since it is *neither the one nor the other*, but rather their common result (to cut—to be cut). (8)

Deleuze's talk of the cut, being cut, is uncannily thematized in *How It Is* in this interchangeability of the active and the passive, the victim and the victimizer, an interchangeability that occurs in the peculiar temporality of both past and future, the temporality, that is, of repetition. What charges the moment of the "event" of torture, the event of the "Othering" of the Other, which reifies the subject as equally Other—and thus as the "same" to borrow from Levinas's *Totality and Infinity*—is that the event of torture is the event of desire: "soon unbearable thump on skull long silence vast stretch of time soon unbearable opener arse or capitals if he has lost the thread YOUR LIFE CUNT ABOVE CUNT HERE CUNT as it comes bits and scraps all sorts not so many and to conclude happy end cut thrust DO YOU LOVE ME" (75). The speaker's unbearable question here, "DO YOU LOVE ME," seems unanswerable. Its importance is in its asking, the positing of a question this muddy, tortured context renders perversely hideous, hideous not because of the brutal conflation of love and torture but because the question threatens to reconstitute the subject in a space where the subject is always already "inconceivable." The uncanny effect of the question is thus produced in this perfect distillation of desire. But desire, as Deleuze suggests, "cannot be attained except at the point where someone is deprived of the power of saying 'I.' Far from directing itself toward an object, desire can only be reached at the point where someone no longer searches for or grasps an object any more than he grasps himself as subject" (*Dialogues* 113). Beckett's narrator thus articulates himself in what may be called, if the logic of Deleuze's formulation is followed, the "half-space" of desire. His is an aporetic desire because, as I have outlined, he inhabits a memoryless and thus a subjectless space, a perfect space, perhaps, for this Deleuzian desire. But his overdetermined question, DO YOU LOVE ME, a question containing and reconstituting the subject-object predication (YOU/ME), indeed, a question that can be asked only within an a priori posited subject-object epistemology, threatens to reconstitute the Other *and thus the subject* even as it acknowledges the impossibility of such a containment.

And indeed part three of *How It Is* seems to thematize this reification of the subjectless subject, this "voice no objection back at last a voice back at last in my mouth my mouth" (106), recording "how it was" (103) in these "indelible traces" (104) of becoming in the mud. Here the speaker still feels the "want of memory" (107) and still articulates his story—and the narrator *is* a teller of stories—in the space of repetition: "another story leave it dark no the same story not two stories leave it dark" (109). But it is a moment of repetition that still fails to mark a progress from or to anything, fails to articulate itself as difference. Repetition here articulates itself always in the now, despite the narrator's insistence on the before Pim, with Pim, after Pim structure: "at the instant I leave Bem another leaves Pim and let us be at that instant one hundred thousand strong then fifty thousand departures fifty thousand abandoned no sun no earth nothing turning the same instant always everywhere" (112). This is a "machined" space of desire where desire is perhaps even without knowledge of itself because it never moves from something to something. In this half-space of desire even acknowledgment of the facticity of desire seems erroneous: "no one here knows himself it's the place without knowledge" (123), "the essential would seem to be lacking" (129); but this lack does not itself become the impetus for desire but simply demarcates the space to mark that lack.

But the narrator of *How It Is* is, as he himself acknowledges, a teller of stories in this curious half-space of desire that is also, to borrow from Blanchot and Benjamin, death's space. The story the narrator tells is articulated by its awareness of its own inability to be told, a tale, in a sense, dead before living because nonsignifying: "of this old tale quaqua on all sides then in me bits and scraps try and hear a few scraps two or three each time per day and night string them together make phrases more phrases the last how it was after Pim how it is something wrong there" (106–7). The refrain "something wrong there," which runs throughout the text, acts to signal the narrator's own distance from the facticity of the story he tells. There may be, as he says, "reason in me yet" (111), but the "old tale" he tells, paratactically fractured beyond reckoning—a fracturing perfectly reflective of the narrator's own subjectivity—seems beyond the pale of reason because beyond the possibility of telling.[8] The narrator here in *How It Is* is thus an inhabitant of the same semiotic space of the Unnamable: his discourse, self or "Other" created, is what functions to encode his sense of self, is what articulates him *as* subject. As that discourse disintegrates or, as is the case here in *How It Is,* as the discourse moves paradoxically toward death (paradoxically because how can a generative discourse record its own end?), the anxiety of nonbeing is articulated. But it is the figure of death itself that (re)composes the subject in his being-toward-death even as it threatens the end of discourse.

I have noted previously the relation between Malone as "playful" subject and death, suggesting that the stories he tells "rehearse," or attempt to rehearse, the death—that is, the moment of nonbeing—he so desires: death for Malone becomes the ultimate object and thus it tempers, and *authorizes,* his narrative project. The relation between storyteller and death in *How It Is* has altered with the curious alteration of the subject. As I posited above, the question DO YOU LOVE ME recomposes the storyteller as it reifies the subject "via" the "creation" of the new subject-object relation; moreover, the question, so strikingly "real" (because so strikingly conventional), is an uncanny interloper in this half-lit world where the logic of love seems so absurdly out of place. I suggest that the "figure" of death here operates in a similar way. There is a sense in which the narrator's utter fear of death—"screams I SHALL DIE" (147)—seems redundant because the story he himself articulates, in which this utter anxiety is enunciated, is told in the space of repetition and thus suggests that to die is merely to die again; more crucially, this anxiety is always already an anticipation of the subject *as* subject-ready-to-die and thus as, at least partially, constituted being. But to suffer, to die, in *How It Is* is to suffer and die in an unlocatable temporality and thus is to die in paradox, for death, as Heidegger reminds us, makes sense only in a temporal condition. It is, as Heidegger notes, death that functions to encode the understanding of the present moment of *Dasein*; death as event in futurity composes our sense of now, even our sense as subject: "we must characterize Being-towards-death as a *Being towards a possibility*—indeed, towards a distinctive possibility of Dasein itself" (*Being and Time* 305).

Blanchot continues from Heidegger and writes in *The Space of Literature:* "Having death within reach, docile and reliable, makes life possible, for it is exactly what provides air, space, free and joyful movement: it is possibility" (97). Death for Blanchot, and indeed Heidegger, is the Other for Deleuze: the possible.[9] But Blanchot theorizes the relation between writing and death that also preoccupied Beckett and thus concerns the narrator here in *How It Is*. Blanchot: "Death is . . . from the start linked to the movement, so difficult to bring to light, of the artistic experience" (124): "The search for a death that would be mine sheds light, thanks to the obscurity of its paths, upon precisely what is difficult in artistic 'realization.' . . . Death must exist for me not only at the last moment, but as soon as I begin to live and in life's intimacy and profundity. Death would thus be part of existence, it would draw life from mine, deep within. It would be made of me and, perhaps, for me, as a child is the child of its mother" (125). And indeed the narrator of *How It Is* feels the enormity of the pressure of death on and in his narrative: his awareness of death, however, has none of the calm of a Rilke or a Mallarmé, or indeed of a Blanchot theorizing death through Rilke or Mallarmé. It is the sheer terror of nonbeing that recomposes the subject, just as the impossibility of losing the self in narrative recomposes Malone: "so things may change no answer end no answer I may choke no answer sink no answer sully the mud no more no answer the dark no answer trouble the peace no more no answer the silence no answer die no answer DIE screams *I* MAY DIE screams *I* SHALL DIE screams good" (147; emphasis added). Indeed, we might posit that it is the utter fear of death, as it recomposes the subject, that composes the subject's sense of himself *as* narrator/writer: it is the anxiety produced by the thought of the end of life—"when the panting stops and this voice to have done with this voice namely this life" (144)—that leads the narrator to deny his status merely as recording "scribe" and assert his anxious primacy as fully articulating voice: "yes my voice yes mine yes not another's no mine alone yes sure yes" (146). Like Benjamin, who in "The Story-teller," writes, "Death is the sanction of everything that the storyteller can tell. He has borrowed his authority from death" (94), the narrator of *How It Is* finds his final authority as he writes the moment toward death. The sign "Death" is encoded by the narrator as a sign of the real and thus instantiates an epistemological *particularity* in this general economy of repetition and simulation: death particularizes and reifies a subject who can perhaps only understand death as simulation, as repeated figure of consolidation.

But, as is true for a great number of Beckett's texts, the final words of the novel threaten this reconstituted subject within the aporia of repetition or, more precisely, the aporia of the repetition of authorial denial. Indeed, it is from within the space of the fear of death, with its seeming concomitant reconstitution of the subject as one-who-shall-die, that the narrator articulates what may be seen as the typical Beckettian narrative/hermeneutic aporia, an aporia articulated most clearly in *Molloy* and *Mercier and Camier*. He denies his narrative and thus denies the facticity of suffering:

> all these calculations yes explanations yes the whole story from beginning to end yes completely false yes
>
> that wasn't how it was no not at all no how then no answer how was it then no answer how was it SCREAMS GOOD
>
> there was something yes but nothing of all that no all balls from start to finish yes this voice quaqua yes all balls yes only one voice here yes mine yes when the panting stops yes (144–45)

This final denial—which may in fact itself be denied in the final lines of the text: "good good end at last of part three and last that's how it was end of quotation after Pim how it is"(147)—throws into suspicion the constitution of the subject even as it curiously constitutes him alone, but *singular,* in his solitude. I have attempted to suggest, following Deleuze and Blanchot, following Heidegger, that it is the categories of love and death that (re)constitute the subject without memory: as they place the subject in the machined assemblage of desire these categories always offer the narrator his subjectivity. Yet the detailed, complicated, machined process of victim/victimizer is denied in the final lines of the text and thus the facticity of suffering *as* desire too is denied: "never crawled no in an amble no right leg right arm push pull ten yards fifteen yards no never stirred no never made to suffer no never suffered no answer NEVER SUFFERED no never abandoned no never was abandoned no so that's life here no answer

THAT'S MY LIFE HERE screams good" (146). And thus the question that heads this discussion is doubled and doubly difficult to answer (perhaps there is indeed "no answer"). As a simulation, and in repetition, the suffering moment is (at least) doubled and endlessly unlocatable. And thus as suffering is denied here in the final lines the question is begged but functions to mask in anxiety the facticity of suffering even in its denial. Death—"I SHALL DIE"—would seem to reconstitute the suffering moment and thus the suffering subject, but it too is (at least) doubled as the narrative repeats again its own state as repeated simulacrum: "that's how it was end of quotation after Pim how it is" (147). And the final three words place the narrator at the present unlocatable moment, again: how it is: *comment c'est/commencez/commencer.* We can perhaps read this final reversal as what Heidegger calls a "falling":

> As falling, everyday Being-towards-death is a constant *fleeing in the face of death*. Being-*towards*-the-end has the mode of *evasion in the face of it*—giving new explanations for it, understanding it inauthentically, and concealing it. Factically one's own Dasein is always dying already; that is to say, it is in a Being-towards-its-end. And it hides this Fact from itself by recoining "death" as just a "case of death" in Others—an everyday occurrence which, if need be, gives us assurance still more plainly that "oneself" is still "living." (*Being and Time* 298)

To begin (*commencer*) again in the "how it is" (*comment c'est*) is not to face and inscribe the present moment of death or nonbeing but is to place the subject in a simulacrum-space that simply repeats the assembled machine of desire, perhaps a desire toward death. The constant movement of this text thus is the constant movement toward nullification, a movement that simultaneously nullifies and reconstitutes the narrating subject as desiring subject in a space where he both is and is not, *again.*

I conclude this book with my reading of *How It Is* because it seems to function as both end and turning point in Beckett's oeuvre. It signals the end of the "novel," the "assassination" of the form as A. Alvarez puts it in his *Samuel Beckett,* and a turn into a prose that articulates itself in a more "minimalist," compressed semiosis. But in its extended thematization of repetition, *How It Is* offers itself as a retrospective (meta)hermeneutic of the previous novels, novels in one way or another participating in its construction. *How It Is* is an extended and microscopic meditation on the semiotics of the subject and thematizes the subject's intimate relation to memory, desire, and writing. But what I think it most powerfully suggests, even as it places the subject in what I call its "simulacrum-space" or its "half-space" of desire, is the power of the writing self, the power of the subject's generative discourse. Beckett's narrators are often seen as being in some way passive victims of an extrasubjective ordering force (the Unnamable) or the victims of spiritual or mental defect that renders their discourse and ontology suspect (Watt). It is, I think, crucial to a reading of *How It Is,* and indeed to the entire oeuvre, to keep in mind the facticity of the narrator, his/its indomitable will-to-narrate, to interpret, to know. It is perhaps too simple to remind the reader that it is the narrating subject in *How It Is* who writes his being-toward-death, who, despite what seems the eternal return of his text-as-quotation, recomposes himself by writing his assemblage of desire, his memory, his death. Indeed, we might read the *recorso* structure of the narrator's being (as writing) as a perverse desire to write the moment toward death, endlessly.

It is, at any rate, crucial to notice how each of the novels immediately preceding *How It Is* in turn problematizes the notions of endings: *Molloy* seems to suggest an endlessly circular structure of hermeneutical pursuit, *Malone Dies* suggests the impossibility of ending, as does *The Unnamable.* Most commentators see these tautologies or aporias as symptomatic or at least productive of absolute ontological despair, primarily, I suggest, because most critics seem endlessly caught up in what Derrida would call the "metaphysics" of the *telos* structure, *telos* leading toward the end, the end in turn signifying enlightenment, finality, perhaps the end of becoming. I have a different view of the Beckettian end, the end in perfect emblem in *How It Is.* I see Beckett's ends, as they place the subject "back" at the beginning, as curious spaces of empowerment. Where to end in the ideologico-religious universe of Beckett would be to end without enlightenment, to end without, as it were, ending, Beckett's narrators reconfigure their endings always as beginnings, placing the subject, even as aporetic or decomposing, back at the moment of his own initial articulation. The narrator's final "how it is" in *How It Is,* like Moran's "It was not midnight. It was not raining," or the Unnamable's "I'll go on," more than instantiations of the treadmill of Dasein, recomposes the beginnings of narrative as the beginning of *Being* and thus as the beginning of signification.

Conclusion

The Dialogical Subject in *Endgame* and the Second Trilogy

> All of old. Nothing else ever. Ever tried. Ever failed. No matter. Try again. Fail again. Fail better.
> —*Worstward Ho*

In *The Literary Work of Art,* Roman Ingarden writes:

> In principle, there can be literary works which do not trouble themselves at all with staying within the bounds of a particular type of object; but precisely because of this, they can make a particular aesthetic impression by representing a world that is actually impossible or one that is full of contradictions, going beyond the limits established by the regional essence of reality. We are then dealing with a grotesque dance of impossibilities (*einem grotesken Tanz von Unmöglichkeiten*). To what extent such an "impossible" world can be exhibited, and what aesthetic value qualities and values it affords, are questions that introduce entirely *new* points of view, which without doubt require strictly regulated bounds for the allowable completion of the spots of indeterminacy. (253)

One purpose of this book has been to theorize the nature of reading (and its concomitant theorizing) in its relation to the novels of Samuel Beckett, novels that articulate themselves in this space of impossibility that Ingarden posits. Such a reading thus instantiates a curious relation between itself and the text that, as I have been at some pains to suggest, often articulates itself in an already implicit self-hermeneutic. The preamble of *The Unnamable* is perhaps the most striking example of an extended (self-)hermeneutic prologue that provides the key thematics of, for instance, subjective locus ("Where now?), temporality ("When now?"), and the logic of beginning ("How proceed?"). What is produced by the hermeneutic reader of Beckett—that reader attuned to the specific ways in which Beckett's texts engage specific hermeneutical questions—is interpretation always aware of its peculiar simultaneity with the "originary" text, always aware of itself as, essentially, a simulacrum of the text because interpretation, in the exegetical sense of the term, is perhaps already anticipated and neutered by the metahermeneutic text. Indeed, simulacra of the originary text are perhaps all that any fundamental reader of Beckett can produce, being aware that the text renders allegorical interpretation ontologically if not epistemologically suspect, perhaps—and this is the crucial point—as suspect as the originary text itself.

And thus I end this study of Samuel Beckett's early to middle novels with as many caveats as firm conclusions. Indeed, the very notion of coming to a conclusion in Beckett seems patently absurd, out of harmony with the reason or logic of the Beckettian aporia or paradox. The almost conventional aporia of the Beckettian conclusion, from the logical contradiction of Moran's "It was not raining" to the Unnamable's "You must go on, I can't go on, I'll go on" (by now a touchstone of the Beckettian problematic), to the aporia of the speaker's denial of his narrative in *How It Is*, articulates the ending, indeed, like the beginning, as a problematic rather than definitional threshold. Endings aside, we notice perhaps more fundamentally that the hermeneutic semiosis of each text precludes the coming to a conclusion so vital for the allegorical—what I have called the "hermetic"—hermeneutic. Each text has articulated a particular hermeneutic problem: *Watt*, the function of "appropriation" and phronesis; *Mercier and Camier*, the relation between narrative, epistemology, and the "dialogical" relation between seemingly disparate semiotic "zones"; *Molloy*, the function and elision of the dialogical principle in the process of coming to an understanding; *Malone Dies*, the hermeneutical function of play; *The Unnamable*, the problematic of the definitional threshold of beginning as hermeneutic obligation; *How It Is*, the function (or effect) of the repeated scene of hermeneutic suffering. If there is an overarching hermeneutic economy at work in these texts it would be that of the dialogical function, that function vital to the scene of (self-)interpretation. Each text, whether in its particular textual economy or as it obliges the hermeneutic reader, employs the dialogical principle if only to deconstruct it. Fixing the "subjectivity" of the hermeneutic speaker of the Beckett text, that subjectivity fundamentally dependent precisely on establishing itself in (aporetic) dialogue, thus proves ultimately impossible as the voice of the subject is itself "impossible." Another way perhaps of understanding this impossibility—indeed an impossibility that I argue is the basis of the purest possibility of *Being*—is as a kind of rearticulation of what Gadamer would call hermeneutic "openness." Each hermeneutic of each text articulates the interpretation in what Gadamer would call a fundamental "openness" rather than in a system of closure: indeed, a Gadamerian reading of the interpretive experience absolutely emphasizes the openness of the experience as it is here that the true hermeneutic self is revealed or experiences *phusis* (self-emergence). Thus the "impossible" problematic of speaking, of being spoken, of speaking *to*, still articulates these texts, still places them firmly within a hermeneutic tradition that emphasizes the facticity and openness of dialogue—however defined and articulated—as the grounds (*arche*) of meaning. This problematic of the aporetic dialogue is continually thematized in dramatic texts concurrent with the trilogy and *How It Is*, especially *Endgame*, and in the later prose narratives as *Ill Seen Ill Said, Worstword Ho,* and especially *Company*.

Here I will examine the process of the production of dialogue in these texts to explore how this thematic articulates, or is articulated in, the later texts. As a drama, *Endgame* articulates itself in a different semiotic context from the novels, but Beckett's profound concern with the dialogical principle still remains and is even more important given the aesthetic context that traditionally privileges dialogue above all else. I suggest that *Endgame* is an elaborate exploration of the *absence* of the dialogical function, that function that works, as Gadamer would have it, in the "in-between" stage of hermeneutical understanding. There is of course dialogue in the play in the mundane sense of the word—and it is dialogue, as Hamm suggests, that keeps Clov "here" (58)—but as Clov also quite rightly suggests, the words making up that discourse may no longer have any meaning: "I use the words you taught me. If they don't mean anything any more, teach me others. Or let me be silent" (44).[1] Without a constitutive language, "world" cannot be disclosed, dialogue cannot be grounded or even posited. In the face of this hermeneutic degree-zero semiology, the characters, and especially Hamm, take refuge in narrative as a way, perhaps, to facilitate the dissipation of the exhausted self that can never achieve its end(game) in this endlessly repeated and endlessly "corpsed" (30) world; yet as narrative functions hermeneutically and epistemologically, it also allows for—perhaps by definition inaugurates—the appearance of the possibility of teleological structuration and of "order." The reader of *Endgame* thus has to make sense of the fact that hermeneutics—the possibility of discovering or stumbling on "meaning" ("We're not beginning to . . . to . . . mean something?" [32])—is something, as is often demonstrated in the play, to be derided or even feared, as it serves as a kind of specter, reminding the characters of their infinite remove from the realm of significance. The opposition of Being-in-narrative and Being-present (onstage, in "life" *now*) reveals a secondary opposition between the hermeneutic of narrative and the hermeneutics of Being. *Endgame* ultimately threatens to decompose the Heideggerean notion of hermeneutics as the hermeneutics of Being by delineating two distinct semiological zones through which the hermeneutic function operates.

And it is this split between modes of being, between an existence now—in the degree-zero semiology of the present—and the existence then—that moment retrievable through narrative—that initiates the primary dialogical function in *Endgame,* that function that operates not, as we might expect, in the exigencies of exchanged communication but in the "resurrection" of the past through narrative, acts of narrative that compel the teller into an active, concretizing role. Hamm's central narrative of the beggar is the clearest and most important example of how the dialogical function in the play proper is subtended into one speaker. This narrative, more than a mere self-consciously undermining metanarrative, attempts to produce the "past" within the present instance of discourse via Hamm's own resurrection of the dialogue. He begins, as the narrative unfolds, to take on the voice of the beggar, to "appropriate"—in the hermeneutical sense of the word—the text of the past, in a sense to lose his own subjective fixity in the dialogical exchange.[2] Consider the multiple roles played by Hamm in the following:

> It was then he took the plunge. It's my little one, he said. Tsstss, a little one, that's bad. My little boy, he said, as if the sex mattered. Where did he come from? He named the hole. A good half-day, on horse. What are you insinuating? That the place is still inhabited? No no, not a soul, except himself and the child—assuming he existed. Good. I enquired about the situation at Kov, beyond the gulf. Not a sinner. Good. And you expect me to believe you have left your little one back there, all alone, and alive into the bargain? Come now! (52)

This sequence highlights the dialogical function that is missing from the quotidian linguistic exchanges of Hamm, of Clov, of the parents. It is a complex discursive play-within-a-play that highlights the absent hermeneutical function of dialogue in the play proper. Hamm here "plays" both parts of himself years previously and of the beggar; he appropriates the voice of the beggar in order to concretize him on stage: "It's my little one, he said" (52). The profound irony of the narrative is that it preserves a more "real" sense of "being" than does the stage business of the "real" play world. This effect is achieved primarily by the emotional resonance of the narrative—a resonance that carries through to the end of the play—but also by the fact of its having been framed as a repeated discursive act: repetition serves pragmatically to highlight the importance of narrative as narrative for Hamm and, moreover, the story of the beggar calls to mind an instance in Hamm's life when real ethical (*phronetic*) action could be taken: "All those I might have helped" (68).

The articulation of meaningful dialogue in narrative serves, however, to consolidate the semiotic void of the present, the present that is constantly thrown into "corpsed" relief by the resurrection of the past. Beckett here articulates a *frame* to be repeated again and again in his career, the speaker as (self)-dividing or divided subject, the speaker divided between temporalities, between states of being. As a result of this division, the subject is a priori thrust into a dialogical position, of listening to the self, speaking to the self, devising the self as at once present and non-self-coincidental. The profound irony of the Beckettian text as it is read through the hermeneutical lens of this dialogic function is that the subject is articulated into a zone that compels dialogue even as it denies its hermeneutic viability. The result of this aporetic dialogical matrix is the ever-retreating narrator, the narrative voice endlessly impossible to locate. Perhaps no other text defines this problematic more precisely than *Company*, the first text of the so-called second trilogy:

> For why or? Why in another dark or in the same? And whose voice asking this? Who asks, Whose voice asking this? And answers, His soever devises it all. In the same dark as his creature or in another. For company. Who asks in the end, Who asks? And in the end answers as above? And adds long after himself, Unless another still. Nowhere to be found. Nowhere to be sought. The unthinkable last of all. Unnamable. Last person. I. Quick leave him. (24)

Company is a text in many ways similar to *How It Is*. It articulates a speaker/hearer/listener/deviser in the split between a (perhaps unlocatable) present and a past illuminated, as in *How It Is*, by a series of brilliantly etched memories. The narrative voice—the voice of the listener attempting to maintain a discrete discourse and grammatical distance from himself—articulates the narrative as a means of achieving "company": "Deviser of the voice and of its hearer and of himself. Deviser of himself for company. Leave it at that. He speaks of himself as of another.

He says speaking of himself, He speaks of himself as of another. Himself he devises too for company" (26). The inscription of company here operates both at once as a method for alleviating the barrenness of the present (much as in *Endgame*) and as the articulation of the grounds (*arche*) for dialogue, for the possibility of meaning. The economy of the narrative is organized around the protracted attempt to "have the hearer have a past and acknowledge it" (34) as a means of facilitating a kind of historical consciousness in what appears to be a split—thus in my terms *dialogical*—subject.

Company is organized by the speaker's attempt to maintain his distance from the listener, as if he were the "deviser" of an ontologically distinct "listener," as an author is the deviser of a character: "Might not the hearer be improved? Made more companionable if not downright human. Mentally perhaps there is room for enlivenment. . . . Might he not cross his feet? On and off. Now left on right and now a little later the reverse. No. Quite out of keeping" (27–28). *Company* thus articulates itself as a meditation on the process of being as the process of creation; or, at least, the speaker would like to facilitate the illusion of his "authorial" distance from the hearer. The text thus constructs a "double-vision" of the speaker, an illusion—crucially—systematically to be stripped away: the speaker speaking of himself as "he" and "you" and simultaneously meditating on himself as aesthetic process and product. This "illusion" of the double self is one that *Company*, perhaps unlike the earlier novels, now seems comfortable in exposing precisely as illusion: while the narrator perhaps articulates the desire to maintain the discrete difference between biography and autobiography, between writing of the other and writing of the self (as other?), the text will not allow this and collapses these discursive categories as it collapses the speaker's attempt to maintain himself independent of himself. The speaker is the hearer, both writer and written: "Devised deviser devising it all for company" (46), but the authority commanding the text, unlike the "they" of *Malone Dies* and *The Unnamable*, is not an extrasubjective force but only the speaker:

> Huddled thus you find yourself imagining you are not alone while knowing full well that nothing has occurred to make this possible. The process continues none the less lapped as it were in its meaninglessness. You do not murmur in so many words, I know this doomed to fail and yet persist. No. For the first personal singular and a fortiori plural pronoun had never any place in your vocabulary. But without a word you view yourself to this effect. (61)

There is a sense in which this late text operates as a kind of hermeneutic of the past novels and perhaps especially of *The Unnamable* and *How It Is*, texts founded on the same hermeneutic semiotic, texts articulating their speakers in remarkably similar postures. What separates this text from the previous ones, and thus what sets it up as a retrospective reading of those texts, is its unflinching presentation of the solitude of the speaker: "And you as you always were. Alone" (63). This text refuses to conclude in aporia but crystallizes the unbearable fact of absolute isolation. *The Unnamable* and *How It Is* articulate their speakers and their relations to the narrator (and narrative) in a continually (un)raveling aporia that renders it impossible to "locate" the speaker's relation to either his temporality or ontological position as speaker. *Company* refuses the comfort of aporia, refuses the complication of textuality and contradiction that masks the brutality of isolation in endlessly repeating scenes of regeneration and decay. Aporia functions, as I suggested in my final chapter, as a curious space of empowerment, recomposes the subject back at the beginning of *Being*, not the end in isolation: these aporetic moments, ultimately, sustain the subject even as they threaten to negate him, perhaps *because* they threaten to negate him. *Company* finally articulates the subject in *telos*, at the end, in solitude, alone.

Beckett's final texts are remarkably "still" texts, texts whose speakers/characters are marked by their physical and mental inactivity. In earlier texts characters were confined to beds, to urns, to mud fields, but their mental lives were almost manic in their productivity. In the later texts, solitude has calcified the subject (I prefer the term "character-object" to describe these narrated beings of the final texts), entombed him or her in texts that leave little room for the articulation of narrative acts that essentially defined the worlds of the earlier narrators. The later texts pull back from the subject, isolating him or her in landscape or in memory, refusing either to allow the character-object voice or to maintain any possible illusion of textual/discursive mastery over "world." These later texts—*Ill Seen Ill Said* (1982), *Worstward Ho* (1983)—maintain the separation of narrator and object; indeed, the object of the text, the old woman of *Ill Seen Ill Said*, the "it" of *Worstward Ho*, is placed under microscopic narrative focus, each detail of physical movement tracked painstakingly through landscape in a painstakingly arid grammar:

> Seated on the stones she is seen from behind. From the waist up. Trunk black rectangle. Nape under frill of black lace. White half

halo of hair. Face to the north. The tomb. Eyes on the horizon perhaps. Or closed to see the headstone. . . . Voidlike calm as always. (*Ill Seen Ill Said* 29)

The narrative function in these late texts has been wrenched from the speaking subject, who now is merely grammatical object; the subject is rendered mute, incapable of speech and of dialogue. Whereas in the earlier texts, especially after *Mercier and Camier,* the narrative function articulated the speaker as it articulated his world, the late texts ruthlessly objectify their characters, articulating them in texts of an enormously restrictive economy. The dialogical function in *Ill Seen Ill Said* thus reverts to the unnamed narrator who objectifies the character-object in an inscribed interrogative discourse; that is, the dialogical function finds its voice in the narrator's attempts to make sense of the character-object. Often in the second trilogy, this exploration takes the form of parodical philosophical interrogations: "How came a cabin in such a place? How came? Careful. Before replying that in the far past at the time of its building there was clover growing to its very walls. Implying furthermore that it the culprit. And from it as from an evil core that the what is the wrong word the evil spread. And none to urge—none to have urged its demolition. As if doomed to endure. Question answered" (8–9).[3]

In many ways *Ill Seen Ill Said* recalls the pretrilogy narrative economy of *Mercier and Camier,* specifically in its careful arrangement of narratological doubt as to the precise ontology of the "world" the text discloses; and this doubt is, as in *Mercier and Camier,* located not in the narrated subject but in the narrator/narrative itself (we have no access to the character-object in *Ill Seen Ill Said*). It is the narrator who indicates that his discourse may in fact contain the "wrong words" (9, 17) to describe the character-object's world; it is the narrator who continually cautions itself "Careful." It is the narrator, perhaps punning on "Eye/I," who suggests the character-object's distance from the perceivable "truth" of things: "The eye will return to the scene of its betrayals" (27). It is, finally, the narrator who acknowledges the impossibility of maintaining the epistemological verity of his character-object, who exposes the fictitiousness of her ontology:

Not possible any longer except as figment. Not endurable. Nothing for it but to close the eye for good and see her. Her and the rest. Close it for good and all and see her to death. Unremittent. In the shack. Over the stones. In the pastures. The haze. At the tomb. And back.

And the rest. For good and all. To death. Be shut of it all. On to the next. Next figment. Close it for good this filthy eye of flesh. What forbids? Careful. (30)

This seems an acknowledgment of the purely imaginary or imaginative status of the character-object, of the narrative itself. The eye as epistemological tool is closed in favor of the eye of imagination, the "I" of the naming/narrating subject who fabricates the character-object as it perceives her.

The final text of the second trilogy, *Worstward Ho,* sees the character-object shimmering between the "real" and the grammatical, as the old question "Who speaks?" is again sounded: "Whose words? Ask in vain. Or not in vain if say no knowing. No saying. No words for him whose words. Him? One. No words for one whose words. One? It. No words for it whose words. Better worse so" (*Worstward Ho* 20). The text seems to suggest a distance between character-object and narrator, but as the above quotation exemplifies, the status of "voice" in this text is never fixed. In fact, we might posit that the dialogical subject of *Worstward Ho* is language itself, a realization confirming Gadamer's formulation: "being that can be understood is language"; the text grounds itself as a continual meditation on its own linguistic possibility, continually calling into question in dialogue its own *arche* and *telos* as language. The speaker and spoken are categories never fully differentiated; the possibility of *being* itself is questioned as is the possibility of temporality. This ontological-existential problematic is illustrated in the opening statement of the text: "On. Say on. Be said on. Somehow on. Till nohow on. Said nohow on" (7). It is as if a new language has to be formulated to begin to articulate this state of (narrative) being, which is a state, as equally, of nonbeing: "Say a body. Where none. No mind. Where none. That at least. A place. Where none" (7). This is a dynamic strikingly reminiscent of the problematic of temporality of *How It Is;* and, it seems, the narrator acknowledges that *Worstward Ho* is a recapitulation of the old ontological themes: "All of old. Nothing else ever. Ever tried. Ever failed. No matter. Try again. Fail again. Fail better" (7).

Worstward Ho places the subject/character-object in the most restrictive narrative economy of this second trilogy. Whereas in *Company* the hint of a past life retrospectively animates the corpsed subject, and in *Ill Seen Ill Said* the ontological uncertainty of the woman ("If only she could be pure figment" [20]) sustains the character-object if only in aporia, the subject in *Worstward Ho* is composed of fragments—bones, head, skull, eyes, hands—gradually coalescing into only the vaguest of images of a man. But even as the text achieves an image, that image is denied: "Say bones. No bones but say bones" (8). The text composes itself in a semiosis of absolute contradiction where language composes itself simultaneously to erase its representational force: "Not now. Know better now. Unknow better now. Know only no out of. No knowing how know only no out of" (11). (How far away are we from the "No knowing. No knowing such things any more" [103] of *Mercier and Camier*?) To perceive here is to misperceive; to know is to "unknow"; to see is to be "misseen." The text's language often turns upon itself to meditate on its own status, acknowledging its own impossibility even as it acknowledges its representational energy: "Worsening words whose unknown. Whence unknown. At all costs unknown. Now for to say as worst they may only they only they. Dim void shades all they. Nothing save what they say. Somehow say. Nothing save they. What they say. Whosesoever whencesoever say. As worst they may fail ever worse to say" (28).

Worstward Ho offers itself as an extended meditation on the impossibility of meaning formation in a discourse that restricts meaning a priori. Yet like the Unnamable, who has only his impossible words to define his paradoxical ontology, the narrator in *Worstward Ho* is "confined" to his language, a language of "worser words for worser still." And it is perhaps this realization that marks these later texts as ultimately concerned with (re)tracing the primary dialogical or linguistic territory of the earlier novels. *Worstward Ho* thus articulates again the fundamental themes of the Beckett oeuvre: the agonizing fact of being in a language that endlessly composes and decomposes the subject. Being in Beckett means existing, finally and forever, in a language

> At bounds of boundless void. Whence no farther. Best worse no farther. Nohow less. Nohow worse. Nohow nought. Nohow on. Said nohow on. (47)

Notes

Introduction

1. See also James Acheson, *Samuel Beckett's Artistic Theory and Practice* (1997); Phil Baker, *Beckett and the Mythology of Psychoanalysis* (1997); Mary Bryden's *Samuel Beckett and the Idea of God* (1998); Jennifer Jeffers, ed., *Samuel Beckett: A Casebook* (1998); Lois Oppenheim, ed., *Samuel Beckett and the Arts* (1999); and Thomas Cousineau, *After the Final No: Samuel Beckett's Trilogy* (1999).

2. Hermeneutics as conversation or dialogue is central to the argument of part three of *Truth and Method:*

> Thus it is perfectly legitimate to speak of a *hermeneutical conversation*. But from this it follows that hermeneutical conversation, like real conversation, finds a common language, and that finding a common language is not, any more than in real conversation, preparing a tool for the purpose of reaching understanding but, rather, coincides with the very act of understanding and reaching agreement. (388)

Hermeneutics as dialogue or conversation is one of few methodologies that allows the reader fully to appreciate his or her role in actualizing or concretizing the text. It is of course part of my interest to explore how Beckett's texts resist the logic of the conversation by decomposing the specular reading subject.

3. See Martin Esslin's "What Beckett Teaches Me," one of few works that addresses the issue of ethics in Beckett directly.

4. In part two of *Truth and Method* Gadamer provisionally applies the concept of phronesis to the hermeneutic act. Gadamer borrows the concept from Aristotle's *Ethics,* where phronesis means moral knowledge as "practical action." Gadamer thus expands the idea into hermeneutics, giving hermeneutics a specifically ethical turn: "This is the point at which we can relate Aristotle's analysis of moral knowledge to the hermeneutical problem of the modern human sciences. Admittedly, hermeneutical consciousness is involved neither with technical nor moral knowledge, but these two types of knowledge still include *the same task of application*" (315).

1. Watt

1. I use the word *disclosure* with a nod toward Heidegger's use of *aletheia* in "The Origin of the Work of Art." The problematic of hermeneutics in Beckett's work—specifically in the characters' own process of interpretation—is not that of imposing meaning but of discovering the failure of "world" to disclose or reveal itself. Concomitant with this difficulty is the characters' own discovery of the intimate relation between hermeneutics and ontology. The Unnamable's "Where now? Who now? When now?" (*Three Novels* 291) is the quintessential Beckettian understanding of hermeneutics as the hermeneutics of *Dasein*, what Heidegger in *Being and Time* calls the "analytic of the existentiality of existence" (62).

2. Richard Begam's analysis of the relation between author and narrator in *Watt* is sophisticated and timely. He argues that an epistemological dilemma arises in the mirroring of author and narrator. Although his analysis is necessary, I suggest that it is also crucial to take note of the *reader* in this process of mirroring.

3. Wolfgang Iser's groundbreaking efforts in *The Implied Reader,* specifically his work on Beckett, are important to any attempt to formulate a "metahermeneutic" reading of Beckett. In his discussion of *Molloy,* Iser writes: "Such texts act as irritants for they refuse to give the reader any bearings by means of which he might move far enough away to judge them. The text forces him to find his own way around, provoking questions to which he must supply his answers" (175).

4. In *Being and Time* Heidegger uses the term "thrownness" (*Geworfenheit*) to articulate the sense of finding oneself simply being in a "definite world" (264); thrownness also puts the self "face to face with the 'nothing' of the world" (321). Thrownness thus is predicated on absolute anxiety.

5. We will see that Gadamer's notion of the self maintaining itself is problematized in his reading of the hermeneutical function of play. This is the subject of my reading of *Malone Dies.*

6. Gadamer's philosophical hermeneutics is important to an affective reading of Beckett because it explicitly locates a historical, i.e., actual, reader within the reading dynamic. The historically effected reader is thus one who must engage both the text and the critical reception of the text in the hermeneutical dialogue (we see versions of this process in biblical exegesis). Contrary to the understanding of some of Gadamer's detractors, this appeal to a historically located reader is not an appeal to any essentialist notion of autonomous subjectivity. Gadamer's theorizing the exigencies of reading as translation, his notions of the continually shifting responsibilities of the reader, and his explicitly nonmetaphysical conception of the ontology of text make it clear that Gadamer's hermeneutics is not merely a radical form of theological hermeneutics (although the emphasis on history is common to both). For lucid and energetic explorations of Gadamer's place in the poststructuralist debate on hermeneutics, I refer the reader to Gary Madison's essay "Beyond Seriousness and Frivolity: A Gadamerian Response to Deconstruction" and James Risser's "Reading the Text," both in *Gadamer and Hermeneutics.*

7. I take B(eckett)'s proclamation in "Three Dialogues" that "there is nothing to express, nothing with which to express, nothing from which to express, no power to express, no desire to express, together with the obligation to express" (139) as a starting point for a theorizing of the "obligation" to interpret. Expression—an author's, a character's—has as a necessary and ineluctable concomitant the interpretation of that expression by the reader of the text.

8. I am in agreement with Catharina Wulf, who argues in *The Imperative of Narration* that Watt's increasingly idiosyncratic language reflects a desire to "find a new path which would lead him away from Mr. Knott and the quest for a rational understanding of the latter's world" (45). In *Samuel Beckett*, Steven Connor argues that Watt's difficulties that result from confronting the Nothing that is Knott lead him to "try to do away with language" (35). While Wulf and Connor are not arguing a specifically ethical reading as I am, both their interpretations suggest that Watt's desire is to distance himself from Knott rather than understand him. That understanding—or the attempt—is, as I argue, left to the reader.

9. Although suspicious of allegory, I acknowledge Mary Bryden's reading of Knott-as-subliminal-Yahweh as one that suggests the provisional nature of the reading (*Samuel Beckett and the Idea of God* 36–37). Richard Begam's analysis of similar ideas in *Samuel Beckett and the End of Modernity* is also particularly resonant (78–79).

2. Mercier and Camier

1. The text's reading of itself by way of the summaries is a version of what may be called hermeneutic repetition. The specular nature of the summaries repeats in schematic fashion the structure of the text proper and thus functions as a kind of stabilizing "reading." The semiological effect of repetition will be thematized (again) in *How It Is,* where repetition functions not as stabilizing gesture but to map out a space where the subject can realize itself only as an imitation or simulacrum of itself.

2. The reader is caught in the classic Beckettian paradox where two seemingly exclusive choices must be held together simultaneously: the frisson produced in such an aporia defines the reading experience. S. E. Gontarski, in his essay "*Molloy* and the Reiterated Novel," defines this aporia as a variation of the Cretan's paradox: "Since the narrator insists that his fictions lie, he is telling the truth; therefore, he is lying; therefore, he is telling the truth; therefore, he is lying" (60). It seems to me that Gontarski has defined the paradox nicely here, but it also seems too easy to define the aporia in such seemingly clear terms as "truth" and "lying": the Beckettian narrator moves beyond such binary thinking into what Paul Davies in *The Ideal Real* calls the new "ontology" (see above, chapter 1). There is something other than truth and lying at work in Beckett, something that utterly negates these categories a priori.

3. Barthes's question here is a variation of Foucault's question in "What Is an Author?," itself an acknowledged variation of Beckett's question in *Texts for Nothing 3:* "Leave, I was going to leave all that. What matter who's speaking, someone said what matter who's speaking" (85).

4. In *The Literary Work of Art,* Roman Ingarden discusses the affective power of "spots of indeterminacy" in the "schematic formation" (251) of the text. Ingarden suggests that the literary text is never fully present to itself. And while this suggestive observation is based on a comparison of "real" objects to the textual object (that is, on the fact that they are "ontically" distinct), his suggestion is useful in its application to Beckett's works, which as "schemae" subject the reader to oblique, often incomplete disclosures of elements of plot, to disordered time sequences, and to the absence of useful orientation markers. The literary text, argues Ingarden, is always "in need of further supplementation" (251) on the part of the reader.

3. Molloy

1. This collapsing of the I/you dyad can be seen as a mis-en-abyme of the collapse of the major binary in the novel, that between Molloy and Moran (or the two halves of the novel). Indeed, as Richard Begam points out in *Samuel Beckett and the End of Modernity,* this collapsing of binaries raises crucial questions of ontological priority: "If Molloy and Moran inhabit each other's margins, if each is narrating the other, then where do we locate the antecedent term? Who is the narrator and who is the narrated?" (99).

2. Quoted in Hugh Kenner, *A Reader's Guide to Samuel Beckett* (94).

4. Malone Dies

1. We might compare this formulation of the "purpose" of writing as game to that of the narrator of *Texts for Nothing 7:*

> Another thing, I call that another thing, the old thing I keep on not saying till I'm sick and tired, revelling in the flying instants, I call that revelling, now's my chance and I talk of revelling, it won't come back in a hurry if I remember right, but come back it must with its riot of instants. It's not me in any case, I'm not talking of me, I've said it a million times, no point in apologizing again, for talking of me. (108)

2. In "What Is an Author?" Foucault notes the relation between writing, the game, and subjectivity:

> First of all, we can say that today's writing has freed itself from the dimension of expression. Referring only to itself, but without being restricted to the confines of its interiority, writing is identified with its own unfolded exteriority. This means that it is an interplay of signs arranged less according to its signified content than according to the very nature of the signifier.

Writing unfolds like a game (*jeu*) that invariably goes beyond its own rules and transgresses its limits. In writing, the point is not to manifest or exalt the act of writing, nor is it to pin a subject within language; it is rather a question of creating a space into which the writing subject constantly disappears. (102)

3. Merleau-Ponty, *The Visible and the Invisible*.

5. The Unnamable

1. This is a thematic present again in *Texts for Nothing 5*:
Now I'm haunted, let them come, one by one, let the last desert me and leave me empty, empty and silent. It's they murmur my name, speak to me of me, speak of a me, let them go and speak of it to others, who will not believe them either, or who will believe them too. Theirs all these voices, like a rattling of chains in my head, rattling to me that I have a head. (98)

2. Compare Beckett's discussion of Habit to Coleridge's conception of the function of poetry in the *Biographia Literaria:* poetry "awaken[s] the mind's attention from the lethargy of custom" (chapter 14). In *A Defense of Poetry* Shelley writes: "Poetry lifts the veil from the hidden beauty of the world, and makes familiar objects be as if they were not familiar" (503). Brecht's notion of the function of the *Verfremdungseffekt* and indeed his dramaturgy in general are similar to Beckett's conception of the function of suffering and Shelley's theory of the effect of poetry. In *A Short Organum for the Theatre* Brecht writes: "A representation that alienates is one that allows us to recognize its subject, but at the same time makes it seem unfamiliar. . . . The new alienations [in epic theater] are only designed to free socially-conditioned phenomena from that stamp of familiarity which protects them against our grasp today" (192).

Of course, Coleridge, Shelley, Brecht, and Beckett are drawing on a long line of thinkers theorizing the relation of poetry and any "estranged" discourse to revelatory experience. In chapter 22 of the *Poetics* Aristotle had discussed how metaphor makes the familiar unfamiliar; in the *Novum Organum* (a text surely influential to Brecht) Francis Bacon had discussed the need for "estrangement" in discourse and the "depraved habit" of the understanding which is "necessarily corrupted, perverted, and distorted by daily and habitual impressions" (quoted in Carlson, *Theories of the Theatre* 385).

3. The Unnamable's talk of the "spirit of system" and "method" recalls Coleridge's distinction between these two modes of understanding. In "Essays on the Principle of Method" (in vol. 1 of *The Friend*) Coleridge posits methodical understanding as related to an active, dynamic principle of "progressive transition" (457), a principle in some ways linked to the ethos of the fragment, which in its partial presentation of things initiates the active hermeneutic in the reader, encouraging participation in the progression of understanding. In *The Advancement of Learning* Bacon writes on the aphorism, a mode of discourse related to the

ethos of the fragment; aphorisms "representing a knowledge broken, do invite men to inquire farther" (3:405). Opposed to the principle of method is what Coleridge sometimes calls "system," by which he means a mode of understanding simply articulated as a "dead arrangement" of ideas.

The Unnamable, however, seems to view both the spirit of system and the spirit of method as equally productive of stasis: "The thing to avoid, I don't know why, is the spirit of system" (292): "And yet I despair, this time, while saying who I am, where I am, of not losing me, of not going from here, of ending here. What prevents the miracle is the spirit of method to which I have perhaps been a little too addicted" (303).

An argument could be made that the Unnamable's semiology, in its deliberate removal of any firm narrative signposts, its flouting of any immediately graspable teleology, fits Coleridge's notion of the way in which the discourse of method works. In fact, any reading that participates in some way in the constructing of narrative meaning in this text (as in this chapter) is participating in what Coleridge would call a methodical reading; more precisely, one might posit the Unnamable, himself constructed out of a tissue of discourses and articulated as a *fragment*, as a living embodiment of method.

4. Compare to *Texts for Nothing* 6: "Words, mine was never more than that, than this pell-mell babel of silence and words, my viewless form described as ended, or to come, or still in progress, depending on the words, the moments, long may it last in that singular way" (104).

6. How It Is

1. Ricoeur notes in "The Narrative Function" that the act of narration, as well as reading, is articulated by the narrator's and reader's ability to balance the logic of sequence against the logic of configuration:
> But the activity of narrating does not consist simply in adding episodes to one another; it also constructs meaningful totalities out of scattered events. This aspect of the act of narrating is reflected, on the side of following a story, in the attempt to 'grasp together' successive events. The act of narrating, as well as the corresponding act of following a story, therefore require that we are able *to extract a configuration from a succession.* (278)

But what happens when that configuration is always already a configuration? It is precisely the tension produced as the narrator articulates himself in the interstices of *telos* and the logic of the fragment that defines the narrating subject here as aporetic.

Of course, not all commentators see the problem of parataxis in *How It Is* in these terms. In *Understanding Samuel Beckett,* Alan Astro sees the paratactical structure of the text not as productive of a specifically hermeneutic problematic. Parataxis is for Astro a purely mimetic reflection of the mind's processes: "Beckett in *How It Is* might have gotten far closer to the reality of our thought processes, which are characterized not only by flow but also by gaps. Thus it might be the careful imitation of thought that makes this text so difficult" (105).

2. In *Truth and Method* Gadamer writes:
Moreover, the nature of memory is not rightly understood if it is regarded as merely a general talent or capacity. Keeping in mind, forgetting, and recalling belong to the historical constitution of man and are themselves part of his history and his Bildung. . . . It is time to rescue the phenomenon of memory from being regarded merely as a psychological faculty and to see it as an essential element of the finite historical being of man. (15–16)

For Gadamer, memory is a crucial element in the constitution of the subject *qua* thinking subject: "The process of thought begins with something coming into our mind from our memory" (425).

3. Francis Doherty in *Samuel Beckett* calls these images "retrospective flashes of life" (120) and thus confuses the text's confusion of the relation between past and present. In *Samuel Beckett: A New Approach,* G. C. Barnard suggests that the images construct a memory of past characters such as Sapo and Malone: *How It Is* thus becomes a refrain to the trilogy.

4. Here I follow Gilles Deleuze, who in *The Logic of Sense* defines the simulacrum as built "upon a disparity or upon a difference. It internalizes a dissimilarity" (258); the simulacrum is not a copy (of a copy) but an "image without resemblance" (257).

5. In *Frescoes of the Skull: The Later Prose and Drama of Samuel Beckett,* John Pilling writes: "Part two of *How It Is* is Beckett's most sustained attempt to demolish the distinction between subject and object that has intrigued him all his life" (70). The deconstruction of the subject/object opposition of *Molloy* notwithstanding, I think Pilling somewhat overstates the matter here: it is precisely the relation between desiring subject and inscribable object that is at the heart of the matter.

6. It is tempting to read *How It Is* in part as a political or artistic allegory on the ethics of torture as an ethics of creation, indeed, as Susan Brienza does in *Samuel Beckett's New Worlds*: "Here the situation of all men, and in particular the artist, is presented through an allegory of tormentors and victims either languishing in solitude or locked together in pain" (88). I have suggested in my previous chapters (see especially chapter 1) that such ready allegory can only serve to halt the semiotic process of the text, but I am in full sympathy with the temptation of allegory here in *How It Is,* a text that, at least in one semiotic zone, seems to articulate itself at the boundary of allegory. Why I am in some sympathy with Brienza's allegory is that her frame—like the frame of allegory of reading, for instance—at least acknowledges what I have been calling throughout this project the *facticity* of the text: her allegory acknowledges the facticity of writing and thus orients itself partially toward the actualities and exigencies of text and textuality. Brienza's argument, however, tends again to reify the subject: the fractured semiosis of the narrating subject in *How It Is* is recomposed retrospectively via the

economy of allegory. The narrating subject now *is* the artist and thus the entire epistemo-ontological problematics of the subject is elided.

7. Deleuze and Guattari write: "Every assemblage is basically territorial. The first concrete rule for assemblages is to discover what territoriality they envelop, for there always is one: in their trash can or their bench, Beckett's characters stake out a territory" (503).

8. In "The Novel as Polylogue" Julia Kristeva notes the relation between language and the subject and suggests that a "shattering of language is really a shattering of the body" (162). I have noted that Beckett's narrators function *as* discourse, and thus Kristeva's notion here seems perfectly applicable.

9. In *The Logic of Sense* Deleuze writes that the Other is the "expression of a possible world" (61).

Conclusion

1. Compare Clov's statement to the final proposition in Wittgenstein's *Tractatus*: "What we cannot speak about we must pass over in silence" (7). Wittgenstein, of course, suggests that his propositions—perhaps even the final one—are to be transcended in the process of coming to an understanding: "Anyone who understands me eventually recognizes [the propositions] as nonsensical, when he has used them—as steps—to climb beyond them" (6.54). In Beckett silence may in fact be the final step (it also may be the first step); in any case, for Clov, the possibility of seeing the "world aright" (*Tractatus* 151) is perhaps a "logical" absurdity.

2. I recall Ricoeur's translation of "appropriation" (*Aneignen*) as meaning to "make one's own" what was originally alien. It is crucial to note that appropriation, like the hermeneutical conception of "play," always inaugurates an alteration of the subject: "Appropriation will be the complement not only of the distanciation of the text, but also of the relinquishment of the self" (*Hermeneutics and the Human Sciences* 183).

3. Compare this "debate" to the following passage in *Company,* which sees the narrator theorizing the nature of the "crawling creator." The passage moves with excruciating logic from: "Can the crawling creator crawling in the same create dark as his creature create while crawling?" (52), through a series of agonizing steps until the final: "So while in the same breath deploring a fancy so reason-ridden and observing how revocable its flights he could not but answer finally no he could not. Could not conceivably create while crawling in the same create dark as his creature" (53). There is something satirical about these and other moments of "logic" in Beckett, as if the protracted effort to reach a conclusion in a philosophical context that denies the metaphysics of the conclusion is itself the logical approach to the question of meaning.

Bibliography

Primary Samuel Beckett Sources

Beckett, Samuel. *Company*. In *Nohow On*. New York: Grove, 1995.
———. *Disjecta: Miscellaneous Writings and a Dramatic Fragment*. Ed. Ruby Cohn. New York: Grove, 1984.
———. *Endgame*. Trans. Samuel Beckett of *Fin de Partie* (1957). New York: Grove, 1958.
———. *How It Is*. Trans. Samuel Beckett of *Comment C'est* (1961). New York: Grove, 1964.
———. *Ill Seen Ill Said*. In *Nohow On*. New York: Grove, 1995.
———. *Mercier and Camier*. Trans. Samuel Beckett of *Mercier et Camier* (1970). New York: Grove, 1974.
———. *Proust*. New York: Grove, 1931.
———. *Stories and Texts for Nothing*. Trans. Samuel Beckett of *Nouvelles et Textes Pour Rien* (1955). New York: Grove, 1967.
———. *Three Novels: Molloy, Malone Dies, The Unnamable*. Trans. Samuel Beckett of *Molloy* (1951), *Malone Meurt* (1951), *L'Innomable* (1953). (*Molloy* trans. by Patrick Bowles and Samuel Beckett.) New York: Grove, 1958.
———. *Watt*. London: Picador, 1988.
———. *Worstward Ho*. In *Nohow On*. New York: Grove, 1995.

Other Sources

Abbott, H. Porter. *The Fiction of Samuel Beckett: Form and Effect*. Berkeley: University of California Press, 1973.
Acheson, James. *Samuel Beckett's Artistic Theory and Practice*. Basingstoke, England: Macmillan, 1997.
Alvarez, A. *Samuel Beckett*. 2d ed. London: Fontana, 1992.
Amiran, Eyal. *Wandering and Home: Beckett's Metaphysical Narrative*. University Park: Pennsylvania State University Press, 1993.
Aristotle. *The Nicomachean Ethics*. Trans. J. A. K. Thompson. London: Penguin, 1953.

———. *The Poetics of Aristotle.* Trans. Stephen Halliwell. London: Duckwell, 1987.
Astro, Alan. *Understanding Samuel Beckett.* Columbia: University of South Carolina Press, 1990.
Bacon, Francis. *The Advancement of Learning. Works.* Vol. 3. Ed. James Spedding, Robert Leslie Ellis, and Douglas Denon Heath. London: Longman, 1858–61.
Baker, Phil. *Beckett and the Mythology of Psychoanalysis.* Basingstoke, England: Macmillan, 1997.
Baldwin, Helene L. *Beckett's Real Silence.* University Park: Pennsylvania State University Press, 1981.
Barge, Laura. *God, the Quest, the Hero: Thematic Structures in Beckett's Fiction.* Chapel Hill: University of North Carolina Press, 1988.
Barnard, G. C. *Samuel Beckett: A New Approach, A Study of the Novels and Plays.* London: J. M. Dent, 1970.
Barthes, Roland. "Introduction to the Structural Analysis of Narratives." *The Semiotic Challenge.* Trans. Richard Howard. New York: Hill and Wang, 1988. 95–135.
———. *S/Z.* Trans. Richard Miller. New York: Hill and Wang, 1974.
Bataille, Georges. "Molloy's Silence." *Samuel Beckett's Molloy, Malone Dies, The Unnamable.* Ed. Harold Bloom. New York: Chelsea House, 1988. 13–21.
Baudrillard, Jean. *Simulations.* Trans. Paul Foss, Paul Patton, and Philip Beitchman. New York: Semiotext(e), 1983.
Begam, Richard. *Samuel Beckett and the End of Modernity.* Palo Alto: Stanford University Press, 1996.
Belsey, Catherine. *Critical Practice.* London: Routledge, 1980.
Benjamin, Walter. "The Story-Teller." *Illuminations: Essays and Reflections.* Ed. Hannah Arendt. New York: Schocken Books, 1968. 83–109.
Benveniste, Emile. "The Correlation of Tense in the French Verb." *Problems in General Linguistics.* Trans. Mary Elizabeth Meek. Coral Gables: University of Miami Press, 1971. 205–15.
———. "Language and Human Experience." *Diogenes* 51 (1965): 1–12.
———. "The Nature of Pronouns." *Problems in General Linguistics.* 217–22.
———. "Subjectivity in Language." *Problems in General Linguistics.* 223–30.
Bersani, Leo. "Beckett and the End of Literature." *Samuel Beckett's Molloy, Malone Dies, The Unnamable.* Ed Harold Bloom. New York: Chelsea House, 1988. 51–70.
Blanchot, Maurice. *The Gaze of Orpheus and Other Literary Essays.* Trans. Lydia Davis. Barrytown, N. Y.: Station Hill Press, 1981.
———. *The Space of Literature.* Trans. Ann Smock. Lincoln: University of Nebraska Press, 1982.
———. "Where Now? Who Now?" *Samuel Beckett's Molloy, Malone Dies, The Unnamable.* Ed. Harold Bloom. New York: Chelsea House, 1988. 23–29.

Brecht, Bertold. *A Short Organum for the Theatre: Brecht on Theatre, the Development of an Aesthetic.* Trans. John Willet. New York: Hill and Wang, 1964. 179–205.
Brienza, Susan. *Samuel Beckett's New Worlds: Style in Metafiction.* Norman: University of Oklahoma Press, 1987.
Bryden, Mary. *Samuel Becket and the Idea of God.* Basingstoke, England: Macmillan, 1998.
Buttner, Gottfried. *Samuel Beckett's Novel Watt.* Trans. Joseph P. Dolan. Philadelphia: University of Pennsylvania Press, 1984.
Carlson, Marvin A. *Theories of the Theatre: A Historical and Critical Survey from the Greeks to the Present.* Ithaca: Cornell University Press, 1993.
Cohn, Ruby. *Back to Beckett.* Princeton: Princeton University Press, 1973.
Coleridge, Samuel. *Biographia Literaria: The Collected Works of Samuel Taylor Coleridge.* Ed. James Engell and W. Jackson Bate. Princeton: Princeton University Press, 1983.
———. "On Method." *The Friend: The Collected Works of Samuel Taylor Coleridge.* Vol. 1. Ed. Barbara E. Rooke. Princeton: Princeton University Press, 1969.
Connor, Steven. *Samuel Beckett: Repetition, Theory, and Text.* Oxford: Basil Blackwell, 1988.
Cousineau, Thomas. *After the Final No: Samuel Beckett's Trilogy.* Newark: University of Delaware Press, 1999.
Davies, Paul. *The Ideal Real: Beckett's Fiction and Imagination.* London: Associated University Press, 1994.
Dearlove, J. E. *Accommodating the Chaos: Samuel Beckett's Nonrelational Art.* Durham, N.C.: Duke University Press, 1982.
Deleuze, Gilles. *Dialogues.* Trans. Hugh Tomlinson and Barbara Habberjam. London: Athlone Press, 1987.
———. *The Logic of Sense.* Trans. Mark Lester and Chester Stivale. New York: Columbia University Press, 1990.
Deleuze, Gilles, and Felix Guattari. *A Thousand Plateaus: Capitalism and Schizophrenia.* Trans. Brian Massumi. Minneapolis: University of Minnesota Press, 1987.
de Marinis, Marco. *The Semiotics of Performance.* Trans. Aine O'Healy. Bloomington: Indiana University Press, 1993.
Derrida, Jacques. *Of Grammatology.* Trans. Gayatri Chakravorty Spivak. Baltimore: Johns Hopkins University Press, 1974.
———. *Writing and Difference.* Trans. Alan Bass. Chicago: University of Chicago Press, 1978.
Dettmar, Kevin. "The Figure in Beckett's Carpet: *Molloy* and the Assault on Metaphor." *Rethinking Beckett: A Collection of Critical Essays.* Ed. Lance St. John Butler and Robin J. Davis. London: Macmillan, 1990. 68–88.
Doherty, Francis. *Samuel Beckett.* London: Hutchinson, 1971.

Doll, Mary A. *Beckett and Myth: An Archetypal Approach.* Syracuse, N.Y.: Syracuse University Press, 1988.

Esslin, Martin. "What Beckett Teaches Me: His Minimalist Approach to Ethics." *Samuel Beckett Today/Aujourd'hui: Beckett in the 1990s, Selected Papers from the Second International Beckett Symposium.* Amsterdam: Rodopi, 1993. 13–20.

Federman, Raymond. *Journey to Chaos: Samuel Beckett's Early Fiction.* Berkeley: University of California Press, 1965.

Fletcher, John. *The Novels of Samuel Beckett.* 2d ed. New York: Barnes and Noble, 1970.

Foucault, Michel. "What Is an Author?" Trans. Josue V. Harari. *Textual Strategies: Perspectives in Post-Structuralist Criticism.* Ithaca: Cornell University Press, 1979. 141–60.

Gadamer, Hans-Georg. *Hegel's Dialectic: Five Hermeneutical Studies.* Trans. P. Christopher Smith. New Haven: Yale University Press, 1976.

———. "On the Problem of Self-Understanding." *Philosophical Hermeneutics.* Trans. David E. Linge. Berkeley: University of California Press, 1976. 44–58.

———. *Truth and Method.* 2d ed. Trans. Joel Weinsheimer and Donald G. Marshall. New York: Continuum, 1989.

Gontarski, S. E. "Molloy and the Reiterated Novel." *As No Other Dare Fail.* London: John Calder, 1986. 57–65.

Handwerk, Gary. "Alone with Beckett's Company." *Journal of Beckett Studies* 2 (1992): 65–82.

Harrington, John P. "The Irish Landscape of Samuel Beckett's *Watt*." *Journal of Narrative Technique* 2 (1981): 1–11.

Heidegger, Martin. *Being and Time.* Trans. John Macquarrie and Edward Robinson. New York: Harper and Row, 1962.

———. "The Origin of the Work of Art." *Basic Writings.* Ed. David Farrell Krell. New York: Harper and Row, 1977. 143–87.

Hesla, David K. *The Shape of Chaos: An Interpretation of the Art of Samuel Beckett.* Minneapolis: University of Minnesota Press, 1971.

Hiese, Ursula K. "*Erzahlzeit* and Postmodern Narrative." *Style* 26 (1992): 245–69.

Hill, Leslie. *Beckett's Fiction: In Different Words.* Cambridge, England: Cambridge University Press, 1990.

———. "Fiction, Myth, and Identity in Samuel Beckett's Novel Trilogy." *Samuel Beckett's Molloy, Malone Dies, The Unnamable.* Ed. Harold Bloom. New York: Chelsea House, 1988. 85–94.

Hoffman, Frederick J. *Samuel Beckett: The Language of Self.* Carbondale: Southern Illinois University Press, 1967.

Huizinga, Johan. *Homo Ludens: A Study of the Play Element in Culture.* London: Paladin, 1970.

Hutcheon, Linda. *A Poetics of Postmodernism.* New York: Routledge, 1988.

Ingarden, Roman. *The Literary Work of Art: An Investigation on the Borderline of Ontology, Logic, and Theory of Literature*. Trans. George G. Grabowicz. Evanston, Ill.: Northwestern University Press, 1973.
Iser, Wolfgang. *The Act of Reading: A Theory of Aesthetic Response*. Baltimore: Johns Hopkins University Press, 1978.
———. *The Implied Reader: Patterns of Communication in Prose Fiction from Bunyan to Beckett*. Baltimore: Johns Hopkins University Press, 1974.
———. *Prospecting: From Reader Response to Literary Anthropology*. Baltimore: Johns Hopkins University Press, 1989.
Jacobson, Josephine, and William R. Mueller. *The Testament of Samuel Beckett*. London: Faber and Faber, 1966.
Jameson, Fredric. "Postmodernism and Consumer Society." *Studying Culture: An Introductory Reader*. Ed. Ann Gray and Jim McGuigan. London: Arnold, 1997. 192–205.
Jauss, H. R. "Theses on the Transition from the Aesthetics of Literary Works to a Theory of Aesthetic Experience." *Interpretation of Narrative*. Ed. Mario J. Valdes and Owen J. Miller. Toronto: University of Toronto Press, 1978. 137–47.
Jeffers, Jennifer, ed. *Samuel Beckett: A Casebook*. New York: Garland, 1998.
Katz, Daniel. *Saying "I" No More: Subjectivity and Consciousness in the Prose of Samuel Beckett*. Evanston: Northwestern University Press, 1999.
Kenner, Hugh. *A Reader's Guide to Samuel Beckett*. New York: Farrar, Straus and Giroux, 1973.
Knowlson, James, and John Pilling. *Frescoes of the Skull: The Later Prose and Drama of Samuel Beckett*. London: John Calder, 1979.
Kristeva, Julia. "The Novel as Polylogue." *Desire in Language: A Semiotic Approach to Literature and Art*. Ed. Leon S. Roudiez. New York: Columbia University Press, 1980. 159–209.
Lacan, Jacques. *Ecrits: A Selection*. Trans. Alan Sheridan. New York: Norton, 1977.
Levinas, Emmanuel. *Totality and Infinity: An Essay on Exteriority*. Trans. Alphonso Lingis. The Hague: M. Nijkoff, 1979.
Levy, Eric P. *Beckett and the Voice of Species: A Study of the Prose Fiction*. Dublin: Gill and Macmillan, 1980.
Liddy, James. "Island Truancies: The Saunterings of Mercier and Camier." *Review of Contemporary Fiction* 7 (1987): 44–48.
Madison, Gary. "Beyond Seriousness and Frivolity: A Gadamerian Response to Deconstruction." *Gadamer and Hermeneutics*. Ed. Hugh J. Silverman. New York: Routledge, 1991. 119–35.
———. *The Hermeneutics of Postmodernity: Figures and Themes*. Bloomington: Indiana University Press, 1988.
Marculescu, Ileana. "Beckett and the Temptation of Solipsism." *Journal of Beckett Studies* 11 (1989): 53–64.

Marlowe, Christopher. *The Complete Plays*. Ed. J. B. Steane. London: Penguin, 1969.

Merleau-Ponty, M. *The Visible and the Invisible*. Trans. A. Lingis. Evanston, Ill.: Northwestern University Press, 1968.

Miller, J. Hillis. *The Ethics of Reading: Kant, de Man, Eliot, Trollope, James, and Benjamin*. New York: Columbia University Press, 1987.

———. *Versions of Pygmalion*. Cambridge, Mass.: Harvard University Press, 1990.

Miller, Lawrence. *Samuel Beckett: The Expressive Dilemma*. London: Macmillan, 1992.

Moorjani, Angela. *Abysmal Games in the Novels of Samuel Beckett*. Chapel Hill: University of North Carolina Press, 1982.

———. "A Mythic Reading of *Molloy*." *Samuel Beckett: The Art of Rhetoric*. Ed. Edouard Morot-Sir, Howard Harper, and Dougald McMillan III. Chapel Hill: University of North Carolina Press, 1976.

Morot-Sir, Edouard. "Grammatical Insincerity in *The Unnamable*." *Samuel Beckett's Molloy, Malone Dies, The Unnamable*. Ed. Harold Bloom. New York: Chelsea House, 1988. 131–44.

Murphy, P. J. *Reconstructing Beckett: Language for Being in Samuel Beckett's Fiction*. Toronto: University of Toronto Press, 1992.

Oppenheim, Lois, ed. *Samuel Beckett and the Arts: Music, Visual Arts and Non-Print Media*. New York: Garland, 1999.

Pilling, John. *Samuel Beckett*. London: Routledge and Kegan Paul, 1976.

Pilling, John, and James Knowlson. *Frescoes of the Skull: The Later Prose and Drama of Samuel Beckett*. London: J. Calder, 1979.

Renner, Charlotte. "The Self-Multiplying Narrators of *Molloy, Malone Dies*, and *The Unnamable*." *Samuel Beckett's Molloy, Malone Dies, The Unnamable*. Ed. Harold Bloom. New York: Chelsea House, 1988. 95–114.

Ricoeur, Paul. "Appropriation." *Hermeneutics and the Human Sciences*. Ed. John B. Thompson. Cambridge: Cambridge University Press, 1981. 182–93.

———. "The Hermeneutical Function of Distanciation." *Hermeneutics and the Human Sciences*. 131–44.

———. "Hermeneutics and the Critique of Ideology." *Hermeneutics and the Human Sciences*. 63–100.

———. "The Narrative Function." *Hermeneutics and the Human Sciences*. 274–96.

———. "What Is a Text? Explanation and Understanding." *Hermeneutics and the Human Sciences*. 145–64.

Risser, James. "Reading the Text." *Gadamer and Hermeneutics*. Ed. Hugh. J. Silverman. New York: Routledge, 1991. 93–105.

Robinson, Michael. *The Long Sonata of the Dead: A Study of Samuel Beckett*. London: Rupert Hart-Davis, 1969.

Said, Edward. *Beginnings: Intention and Method*. New York: Columbia University Press, 1975.

Schurman, Susan. *The Solipsistic Novels of Samuel Beckett*. Cologne, Germany: Pahl-Rugenstein, 1987.

Shelley, Percy Bysshe. *A Defense of Poetry*: *Critical Theory Since Plato*. Ed. Hazard Adams. San Diego: Harcourt Brace Jovanovich, 1971.

Smith, Anna. "Proceeding by Aporia: Perception and Poetic Language in Samuel Beckett's *Worstward Ho*." *Journal of Beckett Studies* 3 (1993): 21–37.

Solomon, Philip H. *The Life After Birth: Imagery in Samuel Beckett's Trilogy*. Oxford, Mississippi: Romance Monographs, 1975.

Trezise, Thomas. *Into the Breach: Samuel Beckett and the Ends of Literature*. Princeton: Princeton University Press, 1990.

Watson, David. *Paradox and Desire in Samuel Beckett's Fiction*. London: Macmillan, 1991.

White, Hayden. *The Content of the Form: Narrative Discourse and Historical Representation*. Baltimore: Johns Hopkins University Press, 1987.

Wittgenstein, Ludwig. *Tractatus Logico-Philosophicus*. Intro. Bertrand Russell. London: Routledge and Kegan Paul, 1981.

Wulf, Catharina. *The Imperative of Narration: Beckett, Bernhard, Schopenhauer, Lacan*. Brighton: Sussex Academic Press, 1997.

Credits

The author wishes to thank the following:

Garland Press, for allowing the republication of my chapter "'Speak no more': The Hermeneutical Function of Narrative in Samuel Beckett's *Endgame*," copyright 1998 from *Samuel Beckett: A Casebook*, edited by Jennifer M. Jeffers. Reproduced by permission of Taylor & Francis/Routledge, Inc., http://www.routledge-ny.com

Gordon and Breach Publishers, for allowing the republication of "'A word from me and I am again': Repetition and Suffering in Samuel Beckett's *How It Is*." *LIT: Literature Interpretation, Theory* 9, no. 1 (1998): 85–101.

Rodopi Publishing, for allowing the republication of "'Delicate Questions': Hermeneutics and Beckett's *Watt*." *Samuel Beckett Today/Aujourd'hui* 6 (1997): 149–63.

Grove Atlantic for permitting the quotation of Samuel Beckett's prose.

The Estate of Samuel Beckett and The Calder Educational Trust for permitting the quotation of Samuel Beckett's prose.

Index

Abbott, H. Porter, 4, 21–22, 61, 62
Absurdity, 17
Action, discourse and, 7–10
Aesthetics, 18, 93
Affect, role of, 61–62
Aleatory, tension with order, 42
Aletheia, 112
Allegory, 4, 18; Beckett criticism and, 40; Beckett's parody of, 27–28; of reading, 28; of reading in *Watt*, 36–37
Amiran, Eyal, 61, 110
Anthropomorphization, 21
Aporetic, of metatextual figure, 56
Aporetic dialogue, 2, 126
Aporetic division, 81, 90–91
Aporetic hermeneutic, 3–4
Aporetic subject, 92–93
Aporia: of meaning, 4; in *Molloy*, 78–79; narrative/hermeneutic, 121; of narrator, 56–57; reader's, 9
Appropriation, 74–75; of discourse, 34–35; notion of, 4–5, 20, 88, 142n.2; play as, 88–89; understanding and, 23, 30–31
Aristotelian ethics, 10–11
Aristotle, 7, 9
Artist, 9
Audience, 9
Authority, narrative, 69–70, 121

Bakhtin, 42
Barthes, Roland, 18, 99
Bataille, Georges, 60
Baudrillard, Jean, 115
Beckett's work, modernist and postmodernist experience and, 1–2

Becoming, paradox of, 117
Beginning, 99–100, 106
Being, 53–54, 92, 109–10
Benjamin, Walter, 120–21
Benveniste, Emile, 38–39, 64, 66
Bersani, Leo, 82, 83, 85
Blanchot, Maurice, 85
Brecht, Bertold, 5
Buttner, Gottfried, 22

Characterization, 78–79, 102–3. *See also specific character names*
Characters: obligations of, 8; readers and, 10; subjectivity of, 48
Christ figure, 28, 36
Cohn, Ruby, 41
Coleridge, 139–40n.3 (chap. 5)
Company, 128–30, 132–33
Concretization, 53–54
Connor, Steven, 4, 61, 62
Criticism (on Beckett), 1, 4, 9; on *How It Is*, 110; on *Malone Dies*, 82–86; on *Mercier and Camier*, 40–42, 45; on *Molloy*, 60–63; role of, 3; on trilogy, 59–63; on *The Unnamable*, 93–94; on *Watt*, 21–23, 25, 26–28

Dante, 40, 42
Davies, Paul, 26, 59, 62
Dearlove, J. E., 41, 60
Death, 118–23
Deconstruction, 10
Deictic instability, 71
Deleuze, Gilles, 115–18
Derrida, Jacques, 100

Desire, 115–19; conflation of, 20; and hermeneutics, 17, 38; for order, 39, 41–42, 54
Dettmar, Kevin, 62
Dialogical subject, 124–33
Dialogue: aporetic, 2, 126; ethics of, 2; hermeneutics as, 135n.2; Platonic model of, 9; production of, 126–33; subject in obligatory system of, 2; understanding as, 23
Diegetic/semiotic splitting, of *Mercier and Camier*, 42
Dilemma, 7–9, 97–98
Directedness, 39. *See also* Order
Disclosure, 136n.1
Discours, and *histoire*, 38–40, 42, 45–47, 49–51, 58–59
Discourse: and action, 7–8; appropriation of, 34–35; and ethics, 11; of madness, 35; manipulation of, 45–46; plurality of, 55–56; of realism, 50–51; specular, 38, 58, 73, 106–7; and understanding, 30–31

Ego formation, 20–21
Endgame, dialogical subject in, 124–33
Epistemology, 57, 63–80
Ethics, 7, 10–11; and actions, 9–10; and aesthetics, 93; of dialogue, 2; and discourse, 11; and hermeneutics, 9–10, 102–3; and reading of *The Unnamable*, 92–108; and recognition of Other, 35–36
Ethos, *Three Dialogues* and, 8
Experience, language and, 6, 17

Facticity, of text, 41–42, 141–42n.6
Father figure, 28
Fletcher, John, 40
Form, 22

Gadamer, Hans-Georg: on being in time, 111; on experience and language, 6; on game, 85; on hermeneutical and ethical action, 7; on historically located hermeneutics, 9–10; notion of open indeterminacy, 46; on openness, 125; phenomenological hermeneutic tradition of, 19–20; philosophy of hermeneutics of, 2–5; on play and order, 84; and prejudice, 72; and specular discourse, 106–7; on understanding, 23, 30–31, 34–35, 68–69
Galls incident, 23–24, 26–28
Game, 85, 138n.1 (chap.4), 138–39n.2 (chap. 4). *See also* Play
Godot, 26

Handwerk, Gary, 3
Heidegger, 75, 110, 112; configuration of being in time, 111; notion of thrownness, 19, 136n.4
Heideggerian *Vorgriff*, 72
Hermeneutical action, ethical action and, 9–10
Hermeneutical anxiety, 40. *See also* Desire
Hermeneutical apprehension, of aesthetic object, 18
Hermeneutical conversation, 2
Hermeneutical desire, specular, 38
Hermeneutical dilemma, 97–98
Hermeneutical ethics, 7
Hermeneutical mode of writing, 17
Hermeneutical obligation, 50–51. *See also* Obligation
Hermeneutical principle, 3
Hermeneutical reading, 7
Hermeneutical reflection, 20
Hermeneutical refusal, 31
Hermeneutical relationship, reader/text, 72
Hermeneutical repetition, 137n.2
Hermeneutical subject, 2
Hermeneutical tradition, phenomenological, 19–20
Hermeneutics: of being, 109–11; and desire, 17; development of Watt's, 23–37; as dialogue, 135n.2; and epistemology, 57; Gadamer's philosophy of, 2–5; hermetic, 97; historically located, 9–10; and narrative, 56–57
Hesla, David H., 22
Hill, Leslie, 22, 82, 93, 110
Histoire, discours and, 38–40, 42, 45–47, 49–51, 58–59
Historically located reader, 136n.6

How It Is, 109–23, 129, 130, 132
Huizinga, Johan, 81, 86
Humor. *See* Parody
Hutcheon, Linda, 46

Ill Seen Ill Said, 130–33
Impossibility, 3–4, 124–26, 133
Ingarden, Roman, 53–54
Intergeneric. *See* Intertextuality
Interpretation, blank, 55; obligation of, 137n.7; problematics of, 17. *See also* Hermeneutics
Intertext, tension with text, 42
Intertextuality, 41–42, 54–55; Beckett's use of, 38–39; intratextuality and, 47–49, 55–56; of *Mercier and Camier,* 41, 46–47
Invention, remembrance and, 67–68
Iser, Wolfgang, 19, 62–63, 83
I/you dialectic, 64–69
I/you dyad, in *Molloy,* 138n.1 (chap.3)

Jameson, Fredric, 54–55
Jauss, H. R., 19

Kafka, Franz, 116–17
Kenner, Hugh, 60
Knott, relationship with Watt, 29–37
Knowledge, function of, 43–44

Lacan, Jacques, 20–21, 56
Language: and aporetic dialogue, 2; and experience, 6, 17; structure of, 2–3; and subject, 142n.8; and understanding, 17, 60; in *Watt,* 33–36
Levinas, Emmanuel, 34, 35
Levy, Eric P., 40, 110
Liddy, James, 40
Literary realism, 46
Lying, truth and, 137n.2

Madison, Gary, 6, 8–9, 87
Madness, discourse of, 18, 35
Malone, commentary on own narrative, 81
Malone Dies, 81–91
Marculescu, Ileana, 10
Marlowe, Christopher, 47

Meaning, 8–9; formation of, 20; lack of, 32; narrative object and, 18; obligation and, 8; pursuit of, 17. *See also* Understanding
Memory, 110–15, 141n.2. *See also* Remembrance
Mercier, relationship with Camier, 47
Mercier, Vivian, 26
Mercier and Camier, 38–57; Beckett criticism on, 40–42, 45; diegetic/semiotic splitting of, 42; intertextuality in, 41, 46–47; narrative authority in, 69–70; narrative *discours* in, 42; narrative/hermeneutic aporia in, 121; summaries in, 51–57
Metahermeneutics, 4–5, 18–19, 27, 36
Metanarrative, 41–42; narrative and, 38, 59; as play, 85–88; rhetoric of, 50–51
Metanarrative voice, 46
Metatextual figure, aporetic of, 56
Metatextual moments, 5
Miller, J. Hillis, 8, 9, 100–101
Miller, Lawrence, 61, 93–94
Mirroring, 19, 20, 55–56, 136n.2
Modernist experience, Beckett's work and, 1–2
Molloy, 58–80; aporia in, 78–79; I/you dyad in, 138n.1 (chap.3); narrative/hermeneutic aporia in, 121
Molloy: discourse of narrative of, 71–73; subject position of, 63–70
Moorjani, Angela, 22
Moral knowledge, 9
Moran, 71–73, 77–78
Morot-Sir, Edouard, 93–94
Movement, physical, 130–31

Narcissus, 76
Narration, act of, 63–80, 140–41n.1
Narrative: hermeneutics and, 56–57; Malone's commentary on own, 81; metanarrative and, 38, 39, 59; modes of, 39; narrated and, 39; subjective decomposition and, 75–76; subjectivity and, 48; Unnamable's, 92–93; use of, 56, 131–33
Narrative anxiety, 40. *See also* Desire

Narrative authority, 69–70, 121
Narrative *discours,* in *Mercier and Camier,* 42
Narrative failure, 41–42
Narrative/narrator, ordering, 44–45
Narrative object, meaning and, 18
Narrative voice, 43–46
Narratological zones, 78
Narrator: absence/presence of, 56; aporia of, 56–57; structure of language and, 2–3; as subject, 77–80, 109; subjectivity of, 119
Narrator/narrated, 60

Object-subject relation, 64–69, 141n.5
Obligation, 92–108; of artist and audience, 9; character's, 8; ethical and hermeneutical action and, 9–10; hermeneutic, 50–51, 137n.7; meaning and, 8; reader's, 7–8, 10, 18
Openness, 126
Order, 126–27; desire for, 39, 41–42, 54; play as, 81–82; tension with aleatory, 42. *See also* Reordering
Other, the, 34–36
Othering, 117–20, 142n.9
Ovid, 47

Painting, Watt's reading of, 28–31
Parataxis, problem of, 140–41n.1
Parody, 27–28, 42, 54–55
Personal pronoun, role of, 64–69
Phenomenological hermeneutic tradition, 19–20
Phronesis, 9, 10, 74, 102–3, 105–8, 135n.4
Physical movement, 130–31
Play, 81–91, 142n.2
Poetry, function of, 139n.2 (chap. 5)
Postmodernist experience, Beckett's work and, 1–2
Postmodernist reading of Beckett, 11
Poststructuralist reading of Beckett, 11
Proust, 95–97

Reader: aporia of, 9; character and, 10; distance between specular and actual, 28–29; hermeneutic relationship with text, 72; historically located, 136n.6; manipulation of, 62; obligation of, 7–8, 10, 18; relation between text and, 4–5, 8–9; self-conscious, 3, 6, 19–20, 59; specular, 6–7, 89
Reading: act of, 140–41n.1; allegory of, in *Watt,* 28, 36–37; hermeneutic, 7, 22–23; problematics of, 9; process of, 4, 18–19
Reading subject, 4, 5, 10
Realism, discourse of, 50–51; literary, 46
Recognition, of Other, 35–36
Reflective hermeneutics, 20
Remembrance, 67–68, 75. *See also* Memory
Renner, Charlotte, 82–83
Reordering, in *Watt,* 35–36. *See also* Order
Repetition, 110–15, 118; hermeneutic, 137n.2; by Mercier, 50; semiotics of, 109
Revelation, absolute, 112
Rhetoric: manipulation of, 45–46; of metanarrative, 50–51; self-undermining, 45–46
Ricoeur, Paul, 74; on discourse, 34–35; notion of appropriation, 5–6, 20, 88, 142n.2; notion of directedness, 39; phenomenological hermeneutic tradition of, 19
Robinson, Michael, 21

Said, Edward, 99, 106
Schurman, Susan, 41, 44–45
Second trilogy, dialogical subject in, 124–33
Self, aporetic division of, 81
Self-alienation, Being as, 92
Self-articulation, mutual, 3
Self-conscious reader, 3, 6, 7–8, 19–20, 59
Self-dispossession, Moran's, 77–78
Self-formation, 20
Self-reflexivity, 75, 81–91
Semiotics, of death and writing, 118–23; of desire, 115–18; of memory and subjectivity, 110–15
Semiotic zones, 38, 39, 50–51, 78, 141–42n.6

Smith, Anna, 93
Specular: defined, 10–11; use of term, 19–20
Specularity, 5, 55–56; discourse of, 38, 58, 73, 106–7; Lacanian model of, 56
Specular reader, 6, 89; dismantling of, 77–80; obligations of, 6–7; Watt as, 28–29
Specular subject, 64. *See also* Specular reader
Spirit of system, spirit of method and, 139–40n.3 (chap. 5)
Subject: alteration of, 142n.2; aporetic, 92–93; dialogical, 124–33; integrity of, 79–80; language and, 142n.8; narrator as, 63–90; obligation for decentered, 93; in obligatory system of dialogue, 2; play of, 4; reading, 4, 10; specular, 64; suffering and, 109–10; textuality of, 4; thematics of, 60; written/writing, narrator as, 109
Subject/character object, 132–33
Subjective decomposition, narrative and, 75–76
Subjectivity, 6; of Beckett's characters, 48; erasure of, 85–86; game, and writing, 138–39n.2 (chap. 4); of narrator, 119; semiotics of, 110–15
Subject-object relation, 64–69, 141n.5
Suffering, 95–97, 108, 110, 114–15; denial of, 121–22; subject and, 109–10
Summaries, in *Mercier and Camier*, 51–57

Temporality, 109, 111–15
Temporal splitting, 65–68
Text: fabrication of, 81; facticity of, 41–42; reader and, 4–5, 8–9, 72; as read object, 59; tension with intertext, 42; theoretical approach to, 6
Textuality, 4, 39

Textual object, aporetic division of self in, 81
"Three Dialogues," 8, 9, 94–95
Thrownness, 19, 75, 136n.4
Torture. *See* Suffering
Tracing, 34–35
Translation, effect on reader in *Watt*, 34–37
Trezise, Thomas, 93
Trilogy, 39–40, 56, 58–80; Beckett criticism on, 59–63. *See also Malone Dies; Molloy; Unnamable, The*
Truth, lying and, 137n.2

Understanding, 23, 30–31; language and, 17, 60; modes of, 139–40n.3 (chap. 5). *See also* Meaning
Unnamable, The, 11, 92–108, 129–30; Beckett criticism on, 93–94
Unnamable, narrative of, 92–93

Waiting for Godot, 48
Watt, 17–37, 48; allegory of reading in, 36–37; language in, 33–36; metahermeneutic reading of, 36; plot of, 17–18; reordering in, 35–36; translation of, 34–37
Watt: development of own hermeneutic, 23–37; metainterpretation of, 27; and painting of fractured circle, 28–31; relationship with Knott, 29–37; as specular reader, 28–29
White, Hayden, 56–57
Witnessing, 31–33, 35–36
Wittgenstein, 93
Worstward Ho, 130–33
Writing: game and, 138n.1 (chap. 4), 138–39n.2 (chap. 4); hermeneutic mode of, 17; semiotics of, 118–23
Written/writing subject, narrator as, 109

Jonathan Boulter is assistant professor of English at Saint Francis Xavier University, Antigonish, Nova Scotia. He specializes in twentieth-century literature.